Bookham in the Twentieth Century

Printed by MILLS & SONS, PRINTERS, LTD., Castle Street, Guildford,
and Published by THE BOOKHAMS SOCIAL SERVICE BUREAU, "Two Oaks," The Park, Bookham.

BOOKHAM

IN THE

TWENTIETH CENTURY

Bill Culley

ISBN 0 9506009 7 0

Published by
Bill Culley, 'Carrick', Leatherhead Road, Bookham,
Leatherhead, KT23 4SJ

With the support of the Leatherhead & District
Local History Society

Cover photograph of St Nicolas Church, Great Bookham,
by Ron Goddard

Printed by J W Arrowsmith Ltd., Bristol.

Contents

List of Illustrations

Cover: St Nicolas Church, Great Bookham
Frontispiece: The cover of the Bookhams Bulletin,
September 1934

Introduction

David Bruce, also a member of the Leatherhead and District Local History Society, suggested that I should investigate and record my findings with regard to the history of Great and Little Bookham during the twentieth century. The area covered, with minor exceptions, will be approximately one and a half square miles; from the station in the north, Kennel Lane in the east; Manor House Lane in the west and just beyond the Leatherhead––Guildford Road to the south.

In 1995, 1996 and 1997 I gave illustrated talks in the Old Barn Hall describing the recent history of the Bookhams in the form of tours of the villages. From these talks the suggestion arose that the information should be produced in book form. The historical information, presented as walks around the area, has been obtained over a number of years, partly from documentary research, but largely from recollections of long-standing Bookham residents.

The present book has been produced with the support of the Leatherhead and District Local History Society, although neither the Society nor the numerous folk who I interviewed are responsible for the information contained in it.

Acknowledgements

I thank everybody who has given me information about the history of the two villages, particularly: Stephen Fortescue, the late Turville Kille, George White, Ernie Hulford, Geoff Griffiths, George Butler, Harry Cobb, Reg Williams, Dr Harrison, Charles Finch, Pat Hammond, May Miller, Barbara Hertsell, Joan Hacker, Jack Barker, Vera Weale, Terry Staff, Bob Stevenson, F C Johnston and Robert Kemp.

From the Leatherhead & District Local History Society, the Record Secretary, Brian Godfrey, gave valuable assistance and Jack Stuttard and Peter Tarplee gave some editorial help.

Reference was also made to:– Surrey County Council Poor Rates for Great Bookham 1904–1926; *The Bookhams Bulletin* from 1932: *Continuity and Change in a Surrey Village – The Bookhams 1870–1914*, a dissertation by Joy Morgan; *Life Begins at 80* by D Joce: various Newsletters and Proceedings of the L&DLHS; Kelly's Directories from 1909 and the Archives of Lloyds Bank.

Margaret Sowerbutts and the late 'Cocker' Lambert allowed me to use a large number of their photographs which were reproduced by Alan Scammell.

I am grateful to all for their help. The responsibility for errors lies with me, of course, and I shall appreciate any corrections that readers send.

Last but by no means least, I thank my wife Ena for not only being so patient through the years of preparation of this work but also for the encouragement that she has given me in carrying out this task.

CHAPTER 1

A Summary of the Recent History of Bookham

At the beginning of the twentieth century life in Bookham was similar to that in other rural areas. Many were employed in farming activities, with the land held by a few wealthy landowners.

The London and South Western Railway came to Bookham in 1885 and from that time people began, slowly at first, to be attracted to the district to commute to and from their place of work. An indication of this trend was the introduction of the large Andrew West houses in Church Road and Little Bookham. These started to be built in 1905 following the sale of what had been farm land. Additionally, the railway enabled people to escape from the unhealthy atmosphere of London for a trip to the pleasant countryside of Bookham.

By the turn of the century there was a slight increase in population and an increase in the range of services in the village that now included a bank, insurance agency, music teacher, architect, veterinary surgeon, a second doctor, a telephone company, draper and a district nurse.

Up until about the time of World War I one of the few occasions when villagers were able to 'let their hair down' was on Guy Fawkes night. Torches were made using ginger beer bottles containing paraffin with a rag wick stuffed in the neck of the bottles. With the torches lit, the guy was carried up the High Street to the Fairfield when the fire was lit and the guy placed on the bonfire. A collection for Guildford Hospital was organised by the Lewer family during the festivities.

The main effect of the 1914–1918 war on the two villages was, of course, the utter sadness and probably great bitterness on the loss of 37 of their beloved men in that campaign. The secondary effect was from the shortage of food that encouraged a large increase in the growing of fruit and vegetables by everyone in the village, including the children.

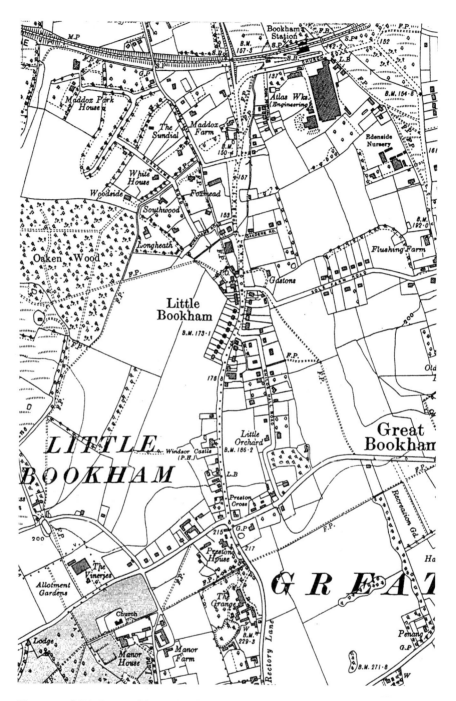

Great and Little Bookham in the 1930s. Crown Copyright, reproduced from the 1934 6" to the mile Ordnance Survey map.

2

Just after the war there were less than ten shops in Bookham, whereas there are around forty today.

The Eastwick Estate, owned by the Keswick family, which had occupied a large part of the village (150 acres in 1914) was sold and became divided in the early 1920s. House building in the Bookhams, though piecemeal in the 1920s and 1930s, was substantially increased following World War II with many housing estates being built after 1950. Most of the roads south of Leatherhead Road were built in the 1930s.

There were two engineering works, one in Little Bookham Street from the early 1900s and the other opposite the station built during World War 1; these provided employment for many for a number of years.

Buses started to run from London to Leatherhead in the early 1920s but did not serve Bookham until the late 1920s or early 1930s. Often when those early buses attempted to climb Hawks Hill the passengers had to disembark and walk with the bus until it reached the top, where they clambered aboard.

According to the *Bookhams Bulletin* of November 1936:

A large amount of interest and strong feeling has been expressed both for and against street lighting. In a referendum, a good majority was in favour of street lighting but then there was the controversy over whether gas or electricity should be used but a majority voted in favour of electricity.

Some side streets had been lit by gas in the mid 1930s but by around 1950 all the street lights were electric.

Before 1900 the Leatherhead Gas and Lighting Company had laid gas pipes to some parts of Bookham but gas was available to the whole area by 1907. Water, supplied by the Leatherhead and District Waterworks Company, was available by 1911 and the Leatherhead and District Electricity Company obtained an order to supply the Bookhams in 1913. Telephones were installed from 1908 by the National Telephone Company. Main sewerage was introduced in 1930.

Voluntary social service in Bookham was carried out by the Bookham Social Services Bureau which was formed in the 1930s. They published the Bookhams Bulletin from 1933 and this is still produced by the Bookham Community Association, the successor to the social services bureau.

During World War II there was an influx of school children evacuees and the departure of many local men and women to serve in one or the other of the services. Later a large number of Canadian troops were to be stationed in the area.

Compared with some of the surrounding areas Bookham received little bomb damage, most occurring in 1940–41. One of the two worst incidents occurred on the 18 September 1940, when a stick of 19 bombs was dropped, the first of them landing on a shop at the Beckley Parade, the remainder dropping in a line towards Polesden Lacey. The second incident was on 19 October when 12 bombs were dropped in a line from Southey Hall to the Leatherhead by-pass causing considerable damage. On a number of other occasions both high-explosive and incendiary bombs fell on Bookham but the majority fell on open ground to the south. In 1944 two V1s landed near the railway, one near Bayfield (now Bookham Grange Hotel) and the other near Maddox Park.

Bookham received several hundred school children evacuees from London, including all of the Strand School at Tulse Hill, for the duration of the war. Mr A.R. Smith, a retired lecturer who lives at West Clandon, was a child evacuee in Bookham. His recollections give an idea of life here at that time. His first guardian was a frail, 73-year-old lady at 3 Shaftesbury Cottages, Little Bookham Street; but he was later moved to 14 Dowlans Road where he was surprised at the length of the gardens compared with those at home. He remembers eating peanut butter from Mrs Hayter's shop at the corner of The Park; the Local Defence Volunteers (later the Home Guard) with pikes, sticks and a farmer's confiscated shot gun; later they were armed with Canadian rifles from the First War; each road had an air raid warden who ensured that black-out regulations were adhered to; most wirelesses were powered by accumulators which needed to be taken to be charged every one or two weeks; most people grew lots of fruit and vegetables and many shot pigeons and rabbits; he recalls walking past a crater near the station in which a bomb was still wedged. Mrs Greville arranged for the Bookham school children to be taken to her garden at Polesden Lacey where they were given a sixpence and saw a Punch and Judy show.

The headmaster of Strand School, Leonard Dawe (known as 'Moneybags' as his initials were LSD), was the commanding officer of the local Army Cadet Force. He used to submit crosswords to the Daily Telegraph, one of which was suspected of containing coded messages for the enemy.

The first prisoners of war to arrive at Bookham were a few Italians who worked at The Mill preparing timber. Following the successful North African campaign many German POWs were to be seen working on the land. Other incomers on the local farms were members of the Women's Land Army with their bright green sweaters and buff coloured jodphurs who were based at Epsom.

At the end of the war Bookham, in common with most places, had its share of street parties.

Over the period covered by this book there were a number of changes in road names, for example:

Lower Road, east of the crossroads, was Eastwick Lane.
Lower Road, west of the crossroads, was Bookham Road.
East street was Back Lane and before that, Fair Lane.
The High Street was known as Upper Street in the early 1900s
Church Road was previously Church Street and before that Lower Street.
Eastwick Road was Eastwick Street.
As the continuation of Church Road developed it became known as New Road more or less north of the Mill. With the coming of the railway, the road was further extended past the station and joined Little Bookham Street near Weale's shop. It was then called Station Road although much later Station Road was abolished and now Church Road and Little Bookham Street meet at the station.

The population growth in the Bookhams is indicated by the following figures:

1871 – 1,286; 1911 – 1,990; 1951 – 4,300; 1981 – 10,300.

CHAPTER 2

High Street and Church Road, South

The building on the north west corner of Guildford Road and the High Street is Rayleigh House, previously the Victoria Hotel. Built in 1896 as a temperance hotel for Mrs Chrystie, a widow who owned much of the village and was an ardent temperance worker. The hotel was built by Andrew West who, in common with Mrs Chrystie, was a native of Fife in Scotland.

Following the death of Mrs Chrystie in 1911, the Victoria Hotel was bought in 1919 by Victor Hayward of The Grove who continued to own it through the 1920s. During the 1920s and 30s there were leisure facilities for the young at the hotel, including a youth club in the basement. The building behind the hotel had a billiard room on the first floor with a cycle store beneath. It continued as a hotel until the mid-1950s, with the exception of 1939-1945 when it was used as a Home Guard headquarters, a British Restaurant and an ARP centre.

By 1943, the threat of invasion was reduced and the Home Guard and the ARP moved out of the Victoria Hotel and the British Restaurant was transferred to the Barn Hall. Then the Victoria Hotel became one of the many places in the area to house Canadian troops where they remained until the end of the war. In the 1930s Mr Macdonald had a hairdressing salon at the front of the hotel but after his war service with the RAF as a barber he moved to Leatherhead Road. Since the mid 1950s the building has been used as commercial offices with a car park where the hotel outbuildings had been. The present name, Rayleigh House, came from the amalgamation of the name of the firm that first occupied it (Ray Heating) and the owner's name (Mr Lee) thus the name Raylee or Rayleigh was formed . It eventually became occupied by a number of firms, one of which is Henshaws the estate agents.

The two picturesque semi-detached, timber framed cottages at nos 30 and 28, High Street are known as Englands and Victoria

South end of Bookham High Street in the early 1930s with the bungalows known as 'Uncle Tom's Cabin' and two sets of houses which were
later converted to shops.

Cottage, although they have also been known as Victoria Cottages
nos 1and 2. Originally, they were part of the Grove Estate and
were probably a single 16th century building standing in about
two acres of land. In the 17th century the south wall was added
complete with fireplace, bressemer, brick oven and the staircase
alongside, that exist today. The northern part, now Victoria
Cottage, has been a separate house since the late 18th century.
Some of the leaded lights of the first floor windows in diamond
panes, have probably survived from the mid 16th century. no 30
continued to be residential until 1965. Mr and Mrs Atkins lived
there at the beginning of the century; Mr Atkins was a gardener at
Eastwick Park while Mrs Atkins made boiled sweets at home. She
went around the village selling the sweets and at weekends he sold
them in the public houses, 12 for a penny, additional sales being
made at the front door of no 30. The Atkins later moved to
Thorncroft in Leatherhead, where he became the gardener.
Afterwards Albert Scott, the Bookham voluntary fire chief, parish
clerk and gardener, occupied no 30 from about 1917 until at least
1939. The cottage was completely refurbished before it was privately occupied from 1960 until 1965 after which it was used as
commercial offices. In 1992 it became Englands House dental

practice and one can see some of the interior of the cottage as the waiting room.

After living in the front part of the Royal Oak, then in Flint Cottage (near where Flint Close is today) William and Emily Amey, whose family can be traced back to the 1700s in Bookham, moved to no 28 High Street in the early 1900s and this became the home of the Amey family for the next 90 years. Mrs Emily Amey, at the death of her husband from consumption and left with three young children, gave much of her time as a cleaner/caretaker to St. Nicolas Church and the Barn Hall from 1906 until she was 85. At this time the floors had to be scrubbed by hand and there were no such things as vacuum cleaners. Her church duties included not only keeping the church clean and tidy but involved carrying the large number of choir robes back to her cottage for laundering, where there was no electricity for ironing, no washing machine and water had to be drawn from the well at the front of her cottage. She also managed to find time to assist the doctor to deliver babies although she was not qualified, but it is understood that the doctor considered her superior to the nurses at a confinement. She died in 1959, aged 95. Her youngest daughter, Miss Ethel Kate Amey, who had been head girl at Bookham school, travelled to India with a family, taking care of their young children. She returned to this country at the outbreak of World War II when she ran the school meal service at the Barn Hall until 1957. She continued to give her services at St. Nicolas Church and the Over 60's Club until she retired in 1964 for a well earned rest; she died in 1992. Victoria Cottage continues to be residential.

The modern flats well back from the High Street were built in the grounds of Fairfield, where there had been a number of outhouses including a barn, which in recent years had housed a squash court. Fairfield is basically an eighteenth century house built in Queen Anne style with a Mansard roof. The name Fairfield was adopted in 1914 when The Hermitage in Lower Road had its name changed from Fairfield. It was probably one of the first substantial houses built of brick in the High Street and, would have been largely self supporting with its 6 acres of land. On the north side of the house there is a window with bars, sealed on the inside, which ventilated what was a brew house. Ale was brewed and drunk in preference to the water from the well that had become polluted.

The Arnetts, a wealthy business family with five unmarried daughters, lived at Fairfield from the beginning of the century

The back garden of Fairfield House in the 1930s.

until the early 1920s. It is said that Mary Jane Arnett, the youngest daughter, introduced the Boy Scout movement to Bookham, she held weekly scout meetings at Fairfield and took the boys to annual summer camp at Worthing. In St. Nicolas' churchyard one of the two gravestones for the Arnett family has the name Mary Jane Arnett, died 1921. Rear Admiral Pudsey Dawson was the owner of Fairfield after the Arnetts until his death in 1936, when his son, Mounsey Dawson continued to live there until it was sold in 1937.

The last private owner of Fairfield was Lord Tucker, a Lord of Appeal. Soon after the war he presided at the trial for treason of William Joyce, known as 'Lord Haw haw', because of the anti-British propaganda which he broadcast from Germany during the war. Joyce was subsequently executed at the Tower of London. Lord Tucker was very kind to the young folk of the village and allowed them to use his squash court. He also allowed a local law student to use his library. Lord Tucker died in 1975.

Fairfield was bought by Hyde the builder and developer and used as offices. The beautiful gardens at the rear were converted to a car park but the views of the house from the road have been opened up with the development.

The next property is thought to have been originally three attached cottages, two of which (nos 18 and 20) remain residential and the third is now a shop. Until 1965 where the solicitor's office is, used to be an open space with access to the rear of the cottages so that carts could drive through to load and unload at the back of the shop. The office was built on to no 22 in 1965 at the same time as part of the land behind the cottages was sold to make a car park for the Royal Oak. The site of the beauty salon was occupied from about 1909 until at least 1919 by Albert Farrow who had a dairy or, as the locals remember it, a creamery. It became a fish shop in the mid-1920s, then a series of grocer's, Frosts in the late 1920s, Page Bros until 1939 and Drakes through the war years and until the 1960s. John, the son of May and Harry Drake, remembers as a school boy helping his parents in the shop and by counting wartime food ration coupons. Then Suffolks introduced the mini market shop and were there until 1970 when they transferred to the top of the High Street, to what is now Rusts. The shop then became a Do It Yourself shop until 1995 when the Beauty Shop from Church Road moved in.

At cottage no 18, there used to be the telephone exchange for The National Telephone Co. until 1932. Mrs Harris, a widow of World War I lived here with her young family of five children and operated the switchboard. The exchange in Church Road was opened in the early 1930s, replacing that at no 18, but Mrs Harris continued at the new building at least until 1940. Downstairs in the house it is still possible to see where the telephone equipment had been and upstairs the plaster and timber framing indicates that this may be one of the oldest buildings in the High Street. The

The Royal Oak in the 1950s. The corrugated roof of the smithy can be seen just beyond Brackenbury's.

outer brickwork of the three cottages disguises a timber-framed house, possibly circa 1400, with a Georgian facade added in the early 18th century. At this time the house was divided into two parts and a large carpenters shop had been built in the back garden. The ground-floor back rooms were added probably in the late 18th. or early 19th century. In 1896 the property was again divided into three parts plus the carpenters shop and, although the carpenter's shop is no longer there, the three cottages have remained the same except that no 22 was later converted to a shop.

The Royal Oak public house was owned by the Swan Brewery of Leatherhead until 1922. The timber and plaster centre of the building is the original 16th century part and the extensions on both sides are probably Victorian. At the rear of the premises were two cottages which have been incorporated into the public house. It was an alehouse until the mid-1950s when it received a spirit licence transferred from a Dorking pub. One of the landlords of the Royal Oak was Sydney Stevenson who managed the public house for 38 years from 1913 until 1951 ably assisted by his wife, particularly while he was serving in France from 1914 until 1917, when he was wounded and brought home. He died, aged 69, in 1951.

Next to Somerfields supermarket there used to be a cottage in part of what is now the Royal Oak car park. This housed a saddlery business started early in the 20th century by Richard Ragge whose family had run a similar business for centuries in Leatherhead. He was the Bookham Parish Clerk for 55 years and died in 1922, aged 91. His daughter, Catharine, married the village blacksmith, George Wyatt, who had the forge on the opposite side of the High Street. James Stemp (or`Shiner'), who had been an apprentice to Ragge, took over the business around 1918. The single storey workshop lay to the rear of the cottage but the trade changed from saddlery to boot and shoe repairs and the Stemp family continued to run the business until the cottage and the workshop were demolished in the late 1960s in order to make the pub car park.

Where Somerfields is there has been a grocery store since the beginning of the century. In the early 1900s it was Underwoods, a general village store which sold almost everything including millinery. In 1909 Walker-Smith, a licensed grocer, took over the shop and provided a superior service and quality. Mr Walker-Smith was killed in World War I but his wife continued to run the shop with Mr Daley as manager until the 1920s. Mr Everitt took over the management until he set up on his own in a shop in Church Road. Mrs Walker-Smith was very popular and also prominent in various village and church activities. The shop continued as Walker-Smith until the 1970s. The building had large wooden doors on the left through which goods were delivered, with a large plate glass window on the first floor. At the rear there was a bracket on which the hoses of the Bookham fire brigade were hung to dry. The manual fire engine used to be kept here until it was moved to Annett's yard opposite. Over the shop doorway was a bell, which was used to call the fire brigade, this was rung every Saturday by a member of the Lewer family as a test. The shop was purchased by International Stores in the 1960s when the shop front was changed. Later it became Gateway and then Somerfields.

Next door is Burpham House which has housed a baker's for the whole of the century. Mr Grantham was the baker until 1915 after which Edward Moss ran the bakery until Mr and Mrs Hanson took over the business in 1930. Mrs Hanson ran the shop on her own after her husband's death until the 1960s when Pearces took over. Until that time Burpham House had been lived in by the baker's family but then the right hand side became an estate agent's office, Norman and Huggins, before being used by Atwood, an insurance broker.

Lloyds Bank is on the corner of Lower Road. This site was occupied from the late 1800s by William Cordingley, a hardware and plumbers shop. In 1912 this became Stevens, a newsagent, stationer and sweet shop, who remained until the building was extended and altered in 1932 for Lloyds Bank. Above the bank, there was a dental surgery, Hyde and Wright, from the 1930s until the 1960s.

At the top of the High Street, on its east side, where Capel's shop stands, there was a 200 year old, double fronted house, Vine Cottage, standing back from the High Street in a large plot extending to East Street. The High Street frontage reached Grove Cottages to the south. Miss Selina Jane Chrystie (Mrs Chrystie's sister-in-law) lived at Vine Cottage from the early 1900s to the mid-1920s. Like her sister she was a staunch temperance supporter who has been described as a kindly woman who carried food beneath her cape which she took to the needy. The last family to live at Vine Cottage was the Waters who had four daughters, the youngest of whom was Elizabeth. In 1950 she walked in her bridal gown, arm in arm with her father, down the High Street to the Church to be married whilst the villagers lined both sides of the road, clapping and cheering. The poor structural condition of Vine Cottage in 1970 caused it to be demolished and replaced by the present shops and car park. What is now Rusts supermarket was originally Suffolk's next door to Capel's the greengrocers. In the grounds at the front to the left of Vine Cottage stood a small tiled wooden black barn until at least the mid-1950s. Next to the barn there was a single storey building complete with chimneys, known as Uncle Tom's Cabin. It was occupied by George Horley, a jobbing smithy, around the end of the last century. He was a vestry clerk who lived in Back Lane (East Street). Next to occupy the building was Mrs Jones who was a dressmaker. Miss Amey recalled wearing, as a little girl, a sailor suit made by Mrs Jones; matching sailor hats came from Nicklins of Dorking, from where a man came weekly in a horse and trap to collect the money. Later the cabin was believed to have been used by Albert Lutman as a butcher's before it was demolished in the early 1930s; the Black Barn remained until the 1950s.

Next, there are the jewellers, florist and Midland Bank. Here, in the early part of the century there were two semi-detached houses with small front gardens and four stone steps leading up to the front doors. The steps were removed and the houses convert-ed and extended into four terraced houses with small front gar-dens around the early 1930s. The third house became a butcher's shop of Albert Lutman when he moved from Uncle Tom's Cabin. He remained there until at least the 1940s; around 1944 C J Fox took the shop over and remained until about 1970. In the 1970s the houses were extended and the present shop fronts fitted, the front gardens had reached roughly to where the line of cream bricks is on the footway.

Similarly the next three shops, the dry cleaners, the sweet shop and the TV shop were originally a terrace of houses, each with a front garden and stone steps up to the front doors. In 1927 Mr Absalom had the front gardens and steps removed and the terrace converted to shops by Andrew West. The first shop was a grocer's run by Alma Absalom, the son of the owner, until 1966, since when it has been a dry cleaners. The middle shop was run by Mr H Absalom, and then his son Ernest, until the 1960s, but although there have been many owners it remains as a sweet shop. The third shop was Hewlins and Hughes, the chemist, who had moved from lower down the road. They remained there until 1960, part of the time Bernard Donner, the optician, used some of the prem-ises. After Hewlins, Crabtree the chemist took over followed by a

East side of High Street in the 1950s. Fox's butchers had been converted from a house in the 1930s whilst the next three shops had been converted in 1927.

launderette in the 1970s, then Robert's freezer shop, Quality Seconds in the 1980s and now C.A.T.S., television retailers.

The butcher's shop that is now Roberts has been a butcher's at least since the early 1900s when it was owned by the Worral family until the early 1960s. The old slaughter house buildings behind the shop are now used as garages. Worrals also grew herbs and vegetables on a piece of land in East Street. Before the 1950s most cattle were locally reared and it would have been a common site to see cattle or sheep being driven along Church Road from the farms in Bookham.

The shop Cachet occupies the site where the Worral family lived until the 1960s. Then it was a greengrocer, Don Capel, until 1970. For the next 10-15 years it was a ladies' outfitters shop, M A Perry. As with the neighbouring properties, there had been a small front garden surrounded by decorative iron railings.

Where the present computer shop is, between the delicatessen and Cachet, there was a wooden building that projected on to the pavement, similar to Robert's butcher's shop. Hewlins and Hughes occupied this before they moved to the shop which is now C.A.T.S. Then Ma Perry (as she was known) had her first shop there in 1930. In 1960 she moved further down the High Street.

Bookham High Street in the 1950s. The wooden building which projects is Ma Perry's shop, next door to Bookham Fisheries.

The projecting building was demolished and a card and gift shop, Eves, operated there until the 1980s, when there followed an assortment of tenants.

The present delicatessen was a house occupied by the Rollinson family from about the mid 1920s until 1953, then by a married daughter May Miller until 1961 when the three houses were converted to shops and their front gardens with their iron railings were removed. The shop where the Rollinson's house was became Reynold's Furnishings, with a connection at the rear to the Victoria Hall where upholstery work was carried out until 1970 when Ambrose Furnishings took over the business until the 1980s. From the opposite side of the road the original construction of the building may be seen. Where Clowns projects on to the pavement a previous generation of the Rollinson family lived and where George Rollinson had a sweet shop in the front room. George ran the shop until about 1909 when it was taken over by Mrs Mary Ann Rollinson who ran it until about 1913 when Mrs Durrant took the shop over. When Mr Absalom senior and his family moved into the district he traded here from 1925 until 1927 before he had the three shops built further up the High Street. In the early 1950s Mrs.Tanner had a delightful tearoom and cafe at the shop but in the late 1950s it became the Bookham Fisheries. In all of that time the shop front remained the same with three awkward steps at the entrance. In 1961 Mrs Perry ran her business from here until the 1980s. It must have been at that time when the shop front was altered and the steps removed.

The shop that is now the Pat-a-Cake teashop was where Mr

Lewer, the village chimney sweep and his family lived from 1910 until the 1960s. Jackson's Bookham Granary then had the property until 1980 when it became Togs, a young children's clothing shop until the present cafe took over.

Next door is Gran Sports. From the early 1900s until the late 1930s this was the architects and insurance office of Mr Richard Lee that he rented from Mrs Chrystie until 1905, when he bought the former blacksmith's premises and used the ground floor as an office. It was here that he had drawn plans for the conversion of the 250-year-old agricultural barn into the Barn Hall in 1905. Later the building was owned by H Allman, an estate agent, before it was bought by Mrs Jackson in 1946. Bookham Granaries, corn and seed merchants, were here from the 1930s until 1980, incorporating Mr Lewer's house next door into a double-fronted shop in 1960. At one time, as well as the usual cornchandlers' products, they stocked fresh Tillingbourne trout, which were kept in a large fish tank.

On the left of the shop is a narrow alley known as Stent's Alley, as it used to lead to Alexander Stent's barber shop which was here from the early part of the century until some time during World War II. As well as having one's hair cut it was possible to place bets with Mr Stent.

The shops, one of which had been Patrick Gardner's Estate Agency until November 1998 and next door Cascade, were, until the 1950s, a double fronted cottage, known as the Old Forge Cottage. The Wyatt family owned the property from the 1880s until 1930 during which time George Wyatt, the blacksmith married the daughter of Richard Ragge the saddler who lived on the opposite side of the road. Since the late 16th century there had been a smithy in this part of the village. It occupied numbers 21 and 23 and had outbuildings stretching to East Street. The enormous raised hearth was about 6 feet in diameter, the chimney of which collapsed in 1987. Among these buildings was an inn called the Old Tavern. In the early 1930s Mrs Allen served teas at the cottage and from about 1933 to 1939 Jackson's Granary used it as a store. The Jarret family who had lived at The Paddocks Cottage in Dorking Road lived in The Old Forge Cottage from 1940 until 1950. One of the daughters is Mrs Brackenbury who, until recently, ran the nearby hardware shop. In the late 1950s The Old Forge Cottage was completely gutted and converted into two shops as exist today. Number 19, Cascade, was R J Clatworthy, radio and television dealers, until the 1980s. Next door was an estate agents.

We now come to Brackenbury's hardware shop. The right hand

side of the site had been Wyatt's smithy, a lean-to building with a cobbled floor and corrugated iron roof which had stood since at least 1873. The blacksmith lived in the adjacent cottage. The remainder of the site was a builder's yard with a small barn at the back. Charlie Pearce, a builder, decorator and undertaker, used the yard and the barn from the beginning of the century whilst living at no 15. In the early 1900s George Balchin, who owned several properties on this side of the High Street, lived there whilst Miss Emily Balchin continued to occupy it from 1909 to the 1920s. In 1924 Annetts, builders and decorators, were occupants until at least 1938. Annetts were also the village undertakers who made and stored coffins in the barn at the back. Funerals were carried out using a hand-drawn bier.

The builder's yard extended round the back of the terrace, nos 11, 13 and 15, which was built in 1884. In the 1920s and 30s Barclay's Bank had a part-time sub-branch in one of the front rooms of no 15 which closed in 1939. Mr Brackenbury senior, was a builder who was next to use the yard while he and his family lived in no 15. Brackenburys sold hardware in a lean-to adjacent to their house before the present shop was built on the site of the builder's yard and forge. The barn is still used for storage. Mrs Brackenbury, the widow of Mr Brackenbury, junior, continued to run the business until 1998.

At no 13 Mr Davis had a hairdressers on the ground floor for about twenty years from the mid 1930s. In 1959 the front gardens and decorative railing and brick walls of nos 13 and 15 were removed and the ground floors converted into shops. Number 15 was first a shoe shop, Valli, then Charrington's coal office before becoming Mann's estate agency.

National Westminster Bank opened a branch at no 13 and they later extended their premises to include no 11. Latterly the bank became a sub-branch before closing completely in 1997. In 1999 Norman and Huggins moved from across the road and opened an estate agency here.

Numbers 9, 7 and 5 were three small houses named Walnut Tree Cottages which were further back from the road than the present shops. In 1938 the first two were demolished and replaced with shops. Number 9 was Donaldsons, a gentlemen's outfitter and is now the Red Cross shop. Where Ashley's card shop is was opened as greengrocers by Mr Cameron who owned the three properties. The third cottage was demolished and replaced by a shop in 1950. This was opened as Heathers, a toy and sweet shop, Heather

The Crown Corner in 1930 with the public house on the right and St Nicolas' lych gate on the left.

being Mr Cameron's daughter. This shop is now a chemist. The first floor of this group is occupied by a hairdresser.

The Crown Inn was recorded in a survey in the 18th century. It was a picturesque old inn with decorated bargeboards and a board on the front advertising 'Good Beds, Luncheons and Dinners Provided'. It was owned at the beginning of the 20th century by Arthur Clapshaw who converted it to a hotel. A horse cab service and a timber business were operated from the inn yard by a member of the Ranger family. The present Old Crown public house was built on the site in 1932 by Hodgsons of Kingston. The new public house had an off-licence which became The Old Crown Grocery Store in 1970, then a florist and in 2000 it is a hairdressing salon.

Diagonally over the crossroads is the estate agent, Patrick Gardner. The west part of the building had been the King's Arms public house, built in the 16th century of brick and flint. During the winter, when the ivy has lost its leaves, the outline of what had once been windows and a door can clearly be seen. The two parts of the building that extend to the corner are extensions made in the latter part of the 19th century. Until 1905 Harry Edser had a baker's shop here and the part of the building that had been the King's Arms became the bakehouse on the ground floor with stores on the first floor, the access to which was by a surviving outside staircase. From 1905 until the early 1920s what had been Edser's corner shop was occupied by Arthur Sayer as a general store and refreshment rooms which were popular with cyclists and walkers coming from the station on their way to Ranmore and Polesden Lacey. From the early 1920s until the mid-1930s this corner shop was an ironmongers run by Mr Cordingley who had moved from a shop opposite in Lower Road. Then the Bookham Paint and Ironmongery Supply occupied the shop until about 1940. Between 1940 and 1945 the WRVS ran a forces canteen here which was mainly patronised by the Canadian soldiers stationed in the village. In the early 1950s Mrs Hind had a teashop where she also sold antiques but since then it has been an estate agent's office. In recent years the upper floor has been used for a variety of purposes including offices. a flat and a play school.

Proceeding down Church Road, butting on to the corner site is the 18th century Wyvern House, note the figure of the wyvern on the roof. Wyvern House was residential until Tuck and Mann, solicitors, occupied part of it from 1960.

Next is The Tyrrells, named after a former owner Francis Tyrrell. It is a 17th century house that has had many alterations and additions,(including a Georgian update), which originally stood in 3 acres of land. It became a doctor's surgery in 1970/71 when Dr Easton, who had lived in Lower Road since the 1930s, practised there until his death in 1991. The single storey addition on the right was the waiting room.

The building now occupied by Watsons the bakers and J S Electrics was Aberdeen House and had been a butcher's shop and living accommodation since the last century. The slaughter houses at the rear of the shop replaced those that were known as the Old Shamyard on the opposite side of Church Road before the Church Cottages were built. Sidney Madge was the butcher from the early 1900s until the early 1950s. He was a long-standing churchwarden at St. Nicolas and can be seen in a photograph of the Duke and Duchess of York when they attended church during their honeymoon at Polesden Lacey in 1923. Whilst Mr Madge was serving in World War I Mr Lutman, a naturalised German, ran the shop for him. In December 1954 Mr Tottman took over the shop and at this time sheep could still be seen being driven around the back of the shop to be slaughtered. At the front of the shop was an attractive veranda with ornamental wrought iron work supported by wooden uprights. When the butcher's closed in the 1960s the ornamental ironwork was removed and the building sub-divided into two shops, first the Walnut Tree Cafe and a drug store and now the bakers and electrical store. The slaughterhouse and the other outbuildings are still at the rear of the shops but are occupied by various other users. The adjoining shop used by David Fuller was built around 1970.

Gothic House, with its Gothic style windows, now an optician and the post office, had earlier been the vicarage. Robert Wood became the owner of Gothic House, although he lived at Flushing Farm, and Gothic House was divided into two shops. Before that the post office had been on the opposite side of the road and in 1910 it moved to the right hand side of Gothic House where it remains today. It was a much smaller shop then with space at the back for the postmen to sort the Bookham mail. Later the entrance was moved to the side of the building because of the increase in traffic. Philip Camp was Bookham's sub-postmaster for 36 years; he retired in 1998. As an RAF officer and bomber pilot he was shot down three times, awarded the D.F.M. and twice Mentioned in Despatches. The last time he was shot down he was taken prisoner and spent the rest of the war years in a prisoner-of-war camp. Philip has been deeply involved with charity work and the Scouts.

The left-hand side of Gothic House was occupied by T H Birch, an electrical engineer, from 1935 until 1950. The village relied upon him for recharging the accumulator batteries that powered their radio sets. Mr Gott became a partner in 1938 when the shop also sold cycles. From 1960 Mrs D Gardiner took over the shop and also sold toys until the 1970s when the opticians came.

Adjacent to Gothic House there used to be a drive to the Rectory which was situated behind where the parade of modern shops are. The Old Rectory was an early 19th century large, three storey Georgian mansion where Jane Austen visited her godfather, the Reverend Samuel Cooke, the Rector of Great Bookham, in 1809 and 1814. The Reverend George Shepheard Bird lived at the Rectory from 1905 until 1926 when he became Vicar of Rowledge. He was the son of Arthur Bird who lived at The Grange, Rectory Lane, Little Bookham. The Reverend Higgins succeeded the Reverend Bird.

The Rectory moved to Flushing Farm in 1926, then to what is now called Bocheham House in Church Road in the early 1930s and finally to its present site in Fife Way.

The Old Rectory was a private house from the early 1930s and after standing empty for a while it was occupied by the Heslop family in the late 1950s who were known for parties starting at eight on Friday evening and finishing with breakfast at six o clock next day. They were the last occupants of the house.

Two sets of modern shops with flats above were built in 1958 in front of the Old Rectory. These were occupied at different times by, among others, Liptons (grocer), Dewhurst (butcher), Coombes (baker), Reeves (greengrocer), Nick Carter (travel agent), Minerva (gifts), Bradbeer (TV and radio), Frost (grocer), Cripps (fishmonger), Mitchell (ironmonger), Davey (butcher), various cafes and Casseldens (shoes). The last of these came here in 1974 although the Casselden family, through three generations, have had a boot and shoe repair business in Crabtree Lane since they moved from Croydon in 1927.

Until the beginning of 1999 these shops were in two parades with a gap through which one could see a cedar of Lebanon tree which survived from the Rectory garden. The tree was damaged during the 1987 gales and it had to be removed. In 1999 further shops were built making one continuous parade. The Rectory building had been demolished in 1961.

Returning to the crossroads, St Nicolas Church is on the east side of Church Road. A church has been here since the 11th century, it has been enlarged and modified over the years. The church was restored in 1885 and in 1897 a lych gate was fitted to commemorate Queen Victoria's Diamond Jubilee. In 1909 an oak screen was erected in memory of Queen Victoria and in 1913 Mr Bird added the south porch in memory of his wife. In the same year the Keswick family presented a new organ to the church in memory of their father, William Keswick, and a year earlier his widow had installed electric lighting in the church. The glass in the chancel window was destroyed during World War II and panels of 15th. century Flemish glass replaced it in 1954.

Near the lych gate was an elm tree which had been planted in 1627; it was felled in 1977 after being affected by Dutch elm disease. Until recently the churchyard also contained a number of walnut trees. The 1914-1918-war memorial in the north east corner of the churchyard has 37 names inscribed on it, among them are some of families referred to in this book. Within the church is a memorial stone with the names of the fifteen who lost their lives in World War II. In 1985 when a gas pipe was being laid through the churchyard to feed the heating system a brick vault was discovered. In July 1990 the vault was investigated and found to be 24 feet by 14 feet and 7 feet to the top of the rounded roof. It contained 16 coffins of the of the Howard family dating from the 16th and 17th centuries.

Church Road showing the cottages occupied by the Ranger family.

In 1885 the priest's vestry had been added and in 1923 the choir vestry was built. In 1979 the Church Room on the north side of the church was added. The wooden shingles on the tower were replaced in 1972 at the same time as the electrical wiring was renewed. At the end of the 20th century the support timbers of the tower were found to need replacing and this was completed in the year 2000.

Beyond the church are Church Cottages, those parallel with Church Road date from the 17th century whilst those at right angles to them are from the 18th century. There were previously four of the earlier cottages but they have now been amalgamated to three. Two members of the Ranger family had each lived in one of them from at least the turn of the century, and for a time ran a newsagency from the house. The later cottages were condemned as being uninhabitable in the 1950s but they were satisfactorily renovated.

Next to Church Cottages is what was the Ranger family home; Miss Elsie Ranger being the last family member to live there. It has been an estate agents' office since then, occupied by Bridgers, Hamptons and now John Wadsworth. Until the 1970s the National Provincial Bank had a sub-branch in the right-hand side and the doorway was where the steps and handrail remain.

The next properties that we come to are the three shops, Unwin's off-licence at no 24, the shoe repairers at no 22 and the

23

jewellery suppliers at no 20. Numbers 24 and 22 were originally two semi-detached, flint-walled cottages, each with six stone steps with wrought iron handrails jutting out on to the pavement. From the early 1900s each set of steps led to a shop about four feet above ground level. At the beginning of the century Walter Wood, a boot maker, occupied no 24 until he moved his business in 1905 to an outhouse at Hop Garden Cottage in Lower Road. Oliver Goldsmith, a popular character, lived in the rear part of the house. He had been a rent collector for Mrs Chrystie from the many properties that she owned in Bookham. He also ran a youth club in the Victoria Hall in East Street, and in the 1930s he was president of Bookham Cricket Club. He was also a very good amateur artist; he died in 1936 aged 74. In 1905 the Capital and Counties Bank Ltd opened a sub-branch at no 24 and the premises became known as Bank Buildings. Mr Wickham was the manager of the bank which closed in 1914 intending to re-open at the end of the war. However, in the meantime, the Capital and Counties Bank had amalgamated with Lloyds Bank which opened a full time branch there until 1932 when they moved to their present position in the High Street. Fords estate agency then took over the shop followed by Legrove who additionally sold books, stationery, sweets and tobacco until the 1950s. The steps were removed and the floor level of this shop lowered when Mrs Capel (Don's mother) had a florist's shop there for a few years before it was Sally Ann, which sold babies' and childrens' clothes. Since then it has been an off-license: Bottletops, then Davisons and then Unwins.

Next door at no 22 Edwin Bates, the postmaster, had a grocer's shop, a post office, an agency for Pullar's of Perth Dye Works, sold talking machines (that played 81/2 inch double-sided records) and medicines from the early 1900s until his death in 1910 when his wife took the shop over until the end of World War I. The Post Office had been transferred in 1911 to Gothic House on the opposite side of the road and was managed by W Cordingley who previously had the plumber's shop at the crossroads. W Everitt, who had been manager at Walker-Smith's in the High Street, bought the shop at no 22 where he and his wife remained until the late 1930s.

The third shop, no 20, was built for Everitt in 1932. At the same time the steps were removed from the front of Everitt's grocer's shop at no 22 and the front half of the shop lowered to ground level. The steps to the rear part of the shop were put in at this time. Everitt extended his business into the third shop, using it for ladies clothing; the two shops were then called Belfast House. In

Church Road, east side showing Belfast House and Trescaw House.

the late 1930s, with the death of his wife, Everitt sold the business to John Irwin who took over the grocery shop and the ladies clothing shop, which was managed by Miss Wyatt. They ran the two shops until the 1960s when the name was changed from Belfast House to Bardolin House. Their living accommodation above the shop became increasingly used as a store, to such an extent that they built the small bungalow to the rear of the shop to live in. Mr Irwin and Miss Wyatt suddenly closed the business in 1960 and moved from Bookham. The bungalow at the rear of the shop continued to be residential until 1997.

In 1960 Bartholemews Cut Glass took over the left-hand shop, followed by Quality Seconds which later moved to the High Street. Then came Gemini, Quins (insurance agents) and finally the shoe repairers, Hobnail and Last. The shop on the right hand side, no 20, became a pet shop in 1965 run by G V Cripps whose brother had the fish shop on the opposite side of the road. The pet shop was later taken over by David Southgate as the Bookham Pet Shop and he remained there until 1997. The shop is now occupied by Cavendish French Ltd, suppliers of fashion accessories.

Trescaw House was occupied from the early 1900s by James Batten, a newsagent, stationer and toyshop. Later his two daughters ran the shop but after the death of one of them the other, with her husband, Mr Stevens, had the shop from about 1910 until 1912 when they moved their business to where Lloyds Bank is today. Mrs Everitt had a children's clothing shop at Trescaw House from 1920 to the 1930s when as Walter Smith it became a boot and shoe shop, where they also did repairs on the premises, until the 1950s. Elizabeth (ladies wear) opened here in the 1960s and remained until the 1970s. The video shop opened in 1985.

Next door, Bank Cottage, was residential until the 1950s when Arnold, estate agent, had it for a while before it became a ladies hairdressers, Louis Fraser, in the 1960s and Nouveau in the 1970s. In 1981, Mr Hedger opened his dental surgery at Bank Cottage.

The small shop next door was the waiting room to the adjacent doctor's surgery in The Croft from the late 1800s until 1923. Later it was converted to a shop and from 1935 until 1971 it was occupied by Frances, a high-class ladies outfitters owned by Mrs and Miss Kleboe who lived at The Croft. An advertisement in the Bookhams Bulletin in September 1949 referred to *Frances from Madam Dee, late of New Bond Street*. The shop subsequently became Image Perfect (office supplies) then a gift shop and later a temporary home for Casseldens in 1999 whilst the new shops were built opposite.

The Croft, the large house that lies back from Church Road, was the home of Dr Eustace Stedman who was related to Mr Stedman, a surgeon, living at Fairfield. Doctor Procter took over the practice in 1894 until he died in 1915, aged 52. He was both physician and surgeon to the village and Medical Officer of Health for Epsom. Dr Procter was the first person in the village to own a motor car and he became Chairman of the Parish Council when it was formed in 1894. It is understood that Mrs Chrystie's benevolence extended to her subsidising the doctor's charges to the poorer people of the village when medicine cost one penny per bottle and the charge for a tooth extraction was one shilling. An air of distinction was given to The Croft by the lamp in the wrought iron archway over the front gate. After Dr Procter's death Mrs Procter moved to Lower Road but continued to own The Croft which she let to Dr Candy who took over the practice in 1917. Dr Candy continued with his practice at The Croft until 1923 when he transferred the practice to Foulis, no 65 Church Road. The Kleboe family occupied The Croft from 1924. A son, Wing Commander P A Kleboe, AFC, DFC, DSO, killed in action at Copenhagen in 1945, aged 28, is buried in St. Nicolas churchyard. The family continued to live at The Croft until 1971 when it was divided into flats.

Next door is Bocheham House where Mrs Eleanor Dyer, a contemporary of Mrs Chrystie, lived. It was the rectory from the early 1930s until it moved to Fife Way.

CHAPTER 3

Church Road

Cross Church Road and the first house is Bookham Gables, or as it was previously known, The Gables. The double frontage of the house, covered by the double pitched roof, is Georgian. The earlier original 16th century house is attached to the south side whilst the two Bookham Gables Cottages in Post House Lane are also older. It is thought that the cottages were once linked to the house as there used to be a passage that could have connected them. When the main part was built in 1820–1830 the original house became the kitchen and staff quarters. The cook and the gardener each lived in one of the cottages. The main entrance to the house used to be in the front, where the door may still be seen, but around 1900 it moved to the present position. On entering here one goes up five steps to the ground floor under which there is a cellar, there are similar steps at the other side of the Georgian house. The kitchen is large and one can see where the kitchen range was installed, now replaced by an Aga stove.

In the 1930s the two cottages came under separate ownership from Bookham Gables and the footpath which gave access to them has since become Post House Lane. The bungalow at the rear of the property was originally a stable block belonging to the Gables. The occupant of the house until 1953 was Mrs Linden, she was followed for a number of years by the Brown family, and until 1998 by Pat Hammond's family.

Continuing along Church Road on the left-hand side we come to Sole Farm House which is the original farmhouse on the Sole Farm Estate, although it was much smaller then than it is today. The name 'Sole' is from the Anglo-Saxon 'sol', meaning 'a muddy pool', since there was a pond at the north side of the house until the mid 1930s, when it was drained. In the 1800s the estate of 350 acres probably extended westward to Buggs Farm at Preston Cross and northwards to Sole Farm Road. It had been a dairy farm until 1905, when it was sold by the Dawnay family and

Church Road with Fife Lodge on the left and Bookham Gables on the right.

bought by Alfred Bird. Just before 1914 the back of the house was considerably extended with eight bedrooms, a conservatory, and a second pitched roof; however, this extension was demolished later and parts of the foundation are still visible. As with many older properties in Bookham the water supply was from a pump and this survives at the back of the house. Inside, the house is beautifully furnished by the present owners, Dr and Mrs Harrison, and there is a fine staircase.

Almost opposite Sole Farm House is Fife Way. Fife Lodge stood at the entrance of Fife Way and was occupied by Mrs Chrystie and her widowed mother-in-law for over 40 years. Mrs Chrystie, whose husband had been killed while serving with the army in India, is remembered as a kind and considerate person, particularly to the poor and underprivileged to whom she would serve hot broth at times of harsh winter weather. In common with her sister-in-law, Miss Chrystie, she was an ardent temperance worker and a supporter of the Band of Hope. Her beliefs persuaded her to buy local inns, close them and then convert them to residential properties imposing a condition that they could not be used again to sell alcohol. She was a manager of Bookham School, checking registers and paying regular visits to inspect work and to listen to singing and recitations by the children. At times Mrs or Miss Chrystie would pay school fees for children of poorer parents. Mrs

28

Chrystie built Victoria Hall in East Street and she organised a Penny Bank in an attempt to encourage people to save what they possibly could from their meagre wages; paying in was made at the Victoria Hotel once a month. Mrs Chrystie must have been a very wealthy woman since in addition to the generous manner in which she helped the less fortunate, she acquired Bookham farmland as it became available on the market and built property on that land. In addition she arranged temperance outings to the seaside by rail from Leatherhead, which was the nearest railway station at that time. Mrs Chrystie died in 1911 and is buried in Bookham churchyard. A contemporary report in the parish magazine states:

Mrs Chrystie lived in Bookham Village and devoted herself, her time, influence and wealth for the good of the community.

She had been a familiar figure in the village, easily identified by the widow's hat that she always wore, giving the impression of a nun.

Mr Alfred Stileman Bostock, a civil servant, occupied Fife Lodge from 1920 until the late 1930s when he moved to Park View. During the early part of the war he was the Evacuation Officer for Bookham; he died in 1944. Fife Lodge stood derelict for some time until the development of Fife Way in the late 1960s when it was demolished.

Where the Park Lodge and Park Court flats now stand there was a horticultural nursery with two semi-detached houses at the front. Mr Longhurst, who worked at the nursery, lived in one of these since the early part of the 20th century. He supplied and laid the original turf for the Bookham Bowling Club's green at the Chrystie Recreation Ground in 1933, financed by the Bookham Social Services Bureau. The nursery closed and Sole Cottage was demolished in the 1960s–70s and the flats here were built.

Over the road is the Old Barn Hall. Sole Farm had several outbuildings including two large barns. Arthur Bird, a J P and a partner in a firm of London solicitors, had moved with his wife and family to The Grange, Rectory Lane, Little Bookham in 1897. He bought the Sole Farm Estate and converted one of the barns into a village hall. He employed Richard Lee as architect and Cummins of Dorking as builder. George Ranger, a Bookham bricklayer, carried out the work. Mr Bird also arranged for the barn to be furnished by Maples who supplied: 4 stained long tables, 150 bentwood chairs, 6 walnut tables and 8 Douglas armchairs. He also gave a cheque for £50 to cover the initial expenses and stated that he had carried out this work because the working man had nowhere to spend his leisure time outside of his home, other than the public house.

A committee of trustees was appointed that included William Keswick MP, the Lord of the Manor of Eastwick, Mr Pickering-Pick, the Rev George Shepheard Bird (Arthur's son and Rector of Great Bookham). The Barn Hall opening ceremony took place on Empire Day, 1906. Management of the hall worked very well until around 1912 when members of the Trust became increasingly unavailable and the Reverend Bird was left to run things by himself until he moved from the district. In 1906 Mrs Amey of Victoria Cottage, was appointed to be caretaker, cleaner and hirer of the hall at 4/6d per week. She kept the hall clean and tidy until her retirement at the age of 85.

One record shows that Miss Keswick, daughter of the local MP, held a meeting of the Anti-Women Suffragettes at the Hall. The Working Men's Club thrived at the Hall so that an annexe was converted for the club's use in 1911; again Richard Lee was the architect. Older members of the village remember the grand dances that took place for the wealthier people of the neighbourhood at the Barn Hall. In the 1930s, the County Library ran a volunteer library service, twice-weekly at the hall.

Mr Bird, at the age of 85, was obliged to hand over the management of the hall to the Parish Council. With the Surrey Review Order of 1933 and the consequent change in local government including the termination of the parish council, the responsibility for the hall was passed to the Leatherhead Urban District Council. In 1939 the hall became an evacuation centre where the W V S, under the control of Mrs Bowen, served hot meals to between 400 and 500 evacuees for which the London County Council were responsible. Miss Amey, the daughter of the former caretaker, was appointed as the cook in charge. Mrs Bowen also became the Billeting Officer for Bookham. Educational time was rationed; the evacuated children alternated with the local children by having their lessons at school in the mornings and did their homework at the Barn Hall in the afternoons. A wartime clinic, operated by Surrey County Council, was held in the cowman's cottage at the rear of the hall until it transferred to Church House in Lower Road. As the Canadian Army came to Bookham in increasing numbers, social evenings were held in the Barn Hall to entertain them several times a week for the remainder of the war. I know of at least one Canadian soldier who married a Bookham girl and continued to live happily in Bookham. Henry Griffiths, the blind organist at St. Nicolas' Church, led a dance band in the 1930s and continued to perform at dances in the Barn Hall throughout the war years and until just a few weeks before his death in 1946. At the end of the war the evacuees returned to their homes and the Surrey County Council took over the running of the school meals service at the Barn Hall for the pupils of Bookham School and for Poplar Road School in Leatherhead.

In 1946 Bookham Grove, which had become vacant, was offered to the village by the Council as a recreation centre but it was turned down by the local community. In 1948 the Bookham Community Association was formed with Dr Waterfield as the first chairman, Mrs Betty Harrison as vice-chairman and Stephen Fortescue as treasurer. The Barn Hall had been partly paid for out of the rates and had been running at a loss and the Leatherhead Urban District Council attempted to persuade the village to buy it. Fortunately Betty Harrison discovered that the hall was registered with the Charities Commissioners and so the council could not sell it. Later the BCA accepted responsibility for the hall from the council with the Constitution that stated:

the Association to be a non-political, non-sectarian organisation based on the Village and for the Village. To provide a meeting place and facilities for physical and mental training, recreation and for social and intellectual development and to foster a community spirit for the achievement of those purposes.

By this time the hall was in need of much repair and in 1948 the B C A held the first Village Day, which is now an annual fund-raising event. In 1956 school meals were no longer served in the hall because facilities were now available at the school, this caused a reduction in income but fund-raising efforts, largely by Mr and Mrs Harrison and Dr Waterfield, enabled the hall to survive. As the hall and B C A began to prosper a wooden hut was built on the south side of the Hall in the early 1960s called the Waterfield Room. Later in the 1960s an extension was built to the south side of the hall and in 1973 the hall was also extended to the north. A year before the hall manager's flat was built together with a room at the rear, known as the Harrison Room.

Set in the front boundary walls of the Barn Hall are 18 cast-iron staddle stones marked *BARTLETT DORKING*. The Dorking foundry was established in 1820 by Bartletts who operated there for 50 years. These are said to have come from the Eastwick Estate.

In 1906 Bird had sold an adjoining plot to Donald Poole on

condition that the property to be built on it would be of a value of not less than £1000. The second large barn was turned through 90 degrees and winched into position to form part of the house on the northern side of the Barn Hall. The house was called Pitscottie and became The Moorings when it was bought by Lieutenant Commander Catto. He remained there until 1927. A number of extensions and outbuildings appeared during the occupation of the property by Braithwaites, an engineering company. After Braithwaites had moved it continued to be used as offices until its demolition in 1998 to enable the construction of the close, known as The Moorings. However, during demolition timber that was a thought to be 300 years old was found to be 'sawn timber of modern dimensions'. This remains a mystery.

Over the road is The Park with a shop on either side built by Oliver Higby in the 1930s. The shop on the left has always been a newsagent and sweetshop. It was managed in the 1950s by Mrs Hayter, a widow in her seventies, who was to be seen each morning at 7am, rain or shine, wrapped in a shawl and a pixie hood, at the station to sell papers to the commuters. Frank Walker took over the shop until it was bought by Forbouys. On the opposite corner the shop was a dairy starting with Norbury Park Dairies, then Curtis Home Dairy and finally in the 1950s Home Counties Dairies. When they closed in the 1970s Frank Walker opened a sports shop here; it is now an art gallery.

Beyond The Park is the telephone exchange built in 1932 to replace the exchange in the High Street, run by Mrs Sarah Harris, who continued in the new exchange until at least 1939. Beyond the telephone exchange are three shops built in the 1930s by Oliver Higby. Worstead House was occupied by Higby as a builder's merchant until the 1960s. Then it was Hall's Maintenance Service (electrical engineers) and since the mid 1970s it has been Sheila's Hair Fashions.

Next door is Rothwell House where Fred Bellows had a hardware shop from the early 1930s until at least the mid-1950s. By the 1960s it was occupied by a veterinary surgeon.

Cochrane House was Ranger's fish and game shop until the 1950s, then Sheila had her first salon here until she moved to Worstead House. It was then used by the beauty salon until they moved to the High Street.

Between Cochrane House and Rothwell House, about where Millside Court is, was a house called Millside where Miss Davis lived until at least 1939. Mr Goodhew, who had the neighbouring coachbuilding business, used the house as a tea room just before

World War II, it was called Millside Tea Rooms. The house was demolished in 1970–71 and flats replaced it.

Behind where Millside Court is now was Classic Foundations Ltd which manufactured corsets here in the 1950s and 1960s. A cluster of wooden buildings that were well back from the road was originally part of the corn and timber business of the Davis family. These had recently been used as garages, stores and small workshops. They were demolished at the beginning of 1997 before the building of Cochrane Court. Also adjacent to the mill there used to be a small brick building which at one time had been a forge. The Sweet Pea shop was built in the 1930s as a coal office for Rangers. Other coal merchants used this office until it was opened as an estate agency by Porter and Smart before they moved to no 1 Church Road.

The slated brick and stone four storey corn mill with cast-iron window frames dates from c.1830 and survives complete with its brick chimney. This was originally a steam powered corn mill operated by the Davis family which, after about 1913 was used to drive a saw mill. The single storey buildings on either side of the mill were a boiler house to the left and an office on the right.

Davis built a house on either side of the mill: Millside which has been described and Mill House, which is now on the corner of Mill Close. Both this house and the mill are now residential properties. During my visit to The Mill in 1994 the owners, Mr and Mrs Firth

The Mill, Church Road.

33

kindly took me on a guided tour of the building when I was able to see indications of where the machinery had been. It has been suggested that some of the corn milling equipment was moved to the steam mill in Cobham.

Arnold Davis, who died in 1909 aged 87, came from Buckinghamshire and his children, Arnold, Edmund, Priscilla and Frederick (a wheelwright) all worked at the mill. In the 1920s, by which time they were in the timber business, the mill building became derelict but it was used by Mr Allen of Bookham Cottage to store corn and seeds. In the Second World War the building was used for filling palliases with straw for use by the army, later Italian prisoners of war used the building for eating and resting while working at the sawmill. In the 1930s the saw mill produced high quality wood for furniture making but in the war they produced wood for railway wagons, railway sleepers, temporary landing strips etc. Ernie Hulford, who had worked at the sawmill since 1935 and lived at Mill House, told me that during the war he arrived at the sawmill each day at 5 a m to light the boiler, he then worked through until 7p m, with just one hour for lunch. In addition, he somehow was expected to serve with the Home Guard. The sawmill closed in 1947 and Cornish Brickworks Ltd took over the site in 1950, producing brick-built fireplace surrounds until the late 1960s when it closed and Mill Close was built on the site.

Just beyond Mill Close are two semi-detached bungalows that were almshouses belonging to the Eastwick Estate which were built in the early 19th century. The cottages were used as a fruiterers shop by Charles Simmons from at least 1905 for about ten years. In 1926 John C Pullen had a greengrocer shop on the left of the building and lived in the right-hand cottage. He ran the shop here for thirty odd years. Mr Leaver had a veterinary surgery here in the late 1960s whilst living in one of the cottages. There are now two separate bungalows again, one of which is called Pullen Cottage.

Crossing the road to Solecote, a road that takes its name from the house that occupied the site until 1965 when it was demolished and the present housing was built. Solecote was one of a number of large elegant houses built by Andrew West on the west side of Church Street and in Little Bookham around 1905. These houses had a number of common characteristics; for example, the front faced south and not the road, there is arched coving above the windows in the living rooms, they had impressive staircases and exterior red toothed brickwork and decorative terracotta ridge tiles were used. All the West houses had large gardens but

Solecote was by far the largest. The house was demolished in 1965 and the Solecote houses were built.

The next in the row of Andrew West houses is Ribblesdale, which has a small shop at the front. The house itself was built in 1905 but the small building that houses the shop was built much earlier, probably in the mid 1880s. I was given my first opportunity to see, admire and appreciate these elegant houses when Margaret Sowerbutts invited me into Ribblesdale a few years ago. This house is almost completely unaltered from the original design, with the exception of the room that was added on to the side of the house and is used as a supplementary store to the shop. The gardens are well maintained. The shop building itself is interesting since it has been used for a number of purposes. For example, during the 1914–18 war the family of one of the staff at the house lived there with his family of thirteen in the two roomed bungalow consisting of one living room and one bedroom. During the 1920s and 1930s it was used as a garage.

Mr Keppel came to live at Ribblesdale in 1939 and remained until the 1950s. A gentleman told me that he recalls having to call on Mr Keppel one day and as he received no reply when he rang the bell at the house he called at the bungalow. When the door was opened he was amazed to see a complete model railway running throughout the building. Margaret opened the craft shop in the out building during the late 1970s and it remains so at the end of the century.

Next door but one to Ribblesdale is another Andrew West built house, named Foulis, that had been the local doctor's residence and surgery since 1923 when the practice was transferred from The Croft by Dr Candy until his tragic death in 1929 aged 49. His successor was Dr Waterfield who gave a lot of his time to the Bookham Community Association and became its first president. He died in 1960 and was followed at this house by Dr Manclark but Dr Bennett was the doctor living at Foulis when the practice moved to the Medical Centre in the centre of the village. It is believed that the pre-fabricated building used as a waiting room was moved to Effingham Golf Club.

We have now reached the Andrew West house on the corner of Church Road and Sole Farm Road known as Farthings. This was initially named Ednam by the Douglas family at the time that they had it built around 1911. The house was occupied by three generations of the Douglas family until it was sold by the two great grandsons, James and Robert, when each of them had a house built within the very large back garden of Ednam. In 1991 Ednam was empty for about six months before it was bought by Mr Darby who had the house thoroughly renovated with some alterations and additions and renamed Farthings. The 100 foot greenhouse, by then a little worse for wear, was demolished and replaced by a large modern greenhouse.

Sole Farm Road was no more than a cart track before the farm was sold in the early 1900s but it served to link Great and Little Bookham villages, although even by 1914, only two houses had been built in the road.

In the latter part of the last century a small group of people could often be seen on Sundays journeying from Dorking to Bookham by pony, donkey cart or by train to Leatherhead and then walking to Bookham. Almost all of them carried bibles and were members of the free churches in Dorking. The Congregational Church in Dorking sponsored the setting up of the Free Church Mission on a plot of ground on the corner of Church Road and Sole Farm Road which had been bought in 1894 for £60. The mission hall of corrugated iron was built on the plot and an adjoining house was erected for the lay preacher, John Ansell, in the 1900s. In 1911 the Free Church Mission became a Congregational Church which moved in 1929 to Eastwick Road, at which time the iron building was demolished. The adjoining house and the iron railings around the site together with the gate to the hall are still there to be seen.

Next to the mission hall site in Church Road is a bungalow called Flushing Cottage in which farm workers of Flushing Farm were housed. At that time it most probably was two semi-detached properties.

On the opposite side of Church Road there is a large house, partly hidden by trees, called Flushing Meadows. Major-General Hughes lived here in the 1950s and in 1957 he was appointed Sergeant-at-Arms in the House of Commons. Lady Hughes continued to live at the house until the 1970s.

Back across the road is Flushing Farm. This had been a farm of 25 acres, now reduced to a garden. The farm house had been built in two parts, the older part is the north side which is thought to date from around 1600, whereas the south side is believed to have been built about two hundred years later. Part of the exterior farm buildings still exist although they appear to be part of next door's property. James Douglas, of horticultural fame, lived here in 1893 when he first came to Bookham from Scotland. Robert Wood, who was an assessor and collector of taxes as well as a farmer, lived at the farm from the early 1900s until about 1930.

Directly opposite Flushing Farm is The Flushings, a house that stands on rising ground almost completely concealed by trees and shrubs. The owner of the farm lived here whilst the manager was at Flushing Farm. This house is older than the farm; its original name was The Fleshings.

Continue northwards along Church Road to the footpath on the left. Where Edenside Road crosses the footpath we turn left and just along on the left is a development called Elmcroft which takes its name from the large house that stood on this site from the early 1900s until the 1970s. It was another Andrew West house where Mr and Mrs Stanley Russell lived from 1918 until the beginning of World War II. The last occupant of Elmcroft before its demolition was Mrs Mary Mackinnon who used to keep goats on the common near her house.

Beside The Orchard a small cul-de-sac of modern dwellings has been built. One of them is occupied by Arthur Baker, aged 89 in 1999, who retired from the Royal Naval Volunteer Reserve in October 1970. Lieutenant-Commander Baker joined the Navy in 1929 and served in minesweepers and trawlers during World War 2. He was awarded the Volunteer Reserve Decoration in 1966 that now lies with his other six medals in a glass case. During his retirement he made more than one request offering his services to the Royal Navy, the last occasion was in 1993 at the age of 83, and he was puzzled at the lack of response to his requests. He loved playing the violin and played in orchestras since the age of 11. At 89 he was extremely fit both physically and mentally and was still playing with the Surrey Philharmonic and the Slater Symphony Orchestras. Until the death of his wife in 1993 he had lived in Eastwick Drive for some fifty years when he moved to his present address.

Just a little further north on the same side of Church Road, now occupied by modern houses, was the site of Alexander House. At the beginning of the last century this was the Great Bookham Convalescent Home. The Matron of the home was Mrs Lee who was the wife of Richard Lee, the architect, who also lived there. When the home closed the house name was changed to The Glade.

On the west side of Church Road, on Edenside Road was the entrance to the Edenside Nursery which became known as The House of Douglas. This occupied about five acres of land that had been part of the former Lonesome Farm. For some 75 years Great Bookham was the home of the Douglas family whose nursery achieved world-wide fame from producing a prodigious number of varieties of border carnations, pinks and auriculas. Three generations of the family ran this enterprise from 1893 until 1967. James Douglas, the founder, was born in Ednam in Scotland but came south early in his working life. His son James, his grandson Gordon and his great grandsons James and Robert were introduced to the nursery business although the great-grandsons decided not to continue with it. When James came to Bookham in 1893 he lived at Flushing Farm then he moved to the house named Edenside which is now an old persons' residence. He later had the house called Ednam built by Andrew West house on the corner of Church Road and Sole Farm Road. The name Ednam was adopted after his birthplace in Scotland; Edenside is near Kelso and was the name given to the nursery, probably because Kelso was where he first saw edged auriculas the flower that made him famous. The nursery occupied more or less the whole of the area on which the Edenside Estate stands today. It closed in 1967 but the family continued to live at Ednam for some time afterwards. The nursery site was compulsorily purchased by the Leatherhead Urban District Council to enable them to build the

Bookham Station in 1950 when there were still goods sidings, a signal box and steam hauled goods trains.

Edenside estate. Before the nursery closed, Gordon Douglas (a grandson) had a 100 foot greenhouse built in the garden of Ednam in order to carry on the auricula tradition of his father and grandfather.

The names of three new roads on the site of what was the nursery are Greathurst End, Beattie Close and Elms Wood, each one named after a long serving flower grower at Edenside Nursery. The large field just beyond the railway tunnel, south of Commonside, is still owned by the Douglas family. Until 1967, turves were cut and brought back to the nursery by horse and cart, placed in layers one above the other and stood for at least 3 years before the compost was used in the nursery.

As the road developed beyond the nursery it was known as New Road. Later, when it was extended further, past the station as far as Weale's shop, it became known as Station Road. More recently, Station Road became Church Road and Little Bookham Street as it is today.

Continuing along the footpath across the common towards the station we come to two semi-detached houses called Merry Court Cottages. These were probably Victorian cottages for the workers on Merrylands Farm; this farm later became known as Lonesome Farm which was of 30 acres owned by Mr Ware from about 1916 until at least 1960. He had been Clerk of the Parish Council for a time. Up until the early 1950s the farmhouse still had gas and oil lighting. In 1967 the Spinney School in Eastwick Drive closed and moved into the Merrylands Farm buildings remaining there until 1980 when it amalgamated with the Manor House School in Little Bookham.

The three bungalows on the east side of Church Road were built when the Eastwick Estate was sold in the early 1920s. With the break up of the Eastwick Estate a group of Bookham people bought Great Bookham Common in 1923 to prevent development of the common and gave it to The National Trust. Soon after, Little Bookham Common and Banks Common were also donated by the local landowners and the two areas Hundred Pound Bridge Wood and The Birches were purchased later. Until about twenty years ago there was no full-time warden but for the last 14 years Ian Swinney has been resident on the common and has carried out and supervised a large number of improvements. During the 1939–45 war a number of bombs fell on the common the craters of which are still visible, there are also remains of triangular anti-aircraft gun pits.

The London and South Western Railway Company built the

railway through Bookham in 1885 when they built the line between Leatherhead and Effingham Junction at the same time as the Guildford 'New' line via Cobham. The reason for the station being one mile from the village centre is because the Lords of the Manors of Fetcham, Bookham and Effingham insisted that it be no nearer the villages. There had been earlier proposals for the line to cross East Street and the High Street but these were rejected. Whilst the railway was being built in Bookham Mrs Chrystie had a thatched refreshment bar constructed by the station for the rail workers.

The station itself is virtually unchanged from the design when it was built and is of the same pattern as the other stations on the line built at the same time. The main buildings are on the down side and the house attached to the station was where the station master lived until recent times. There was a staff of five comprising the station master, two porters, signalman and a ticket clerk. Now there is only a part-time ticket clerk. Mr Winterton, the station master between 1916 and 1932 had the duty, in 1923, of meeting the Duke and Duchess of York as they alighted from the train on their way to stay at Polesden Lacey as part of their honeymoon.

Until 1965 there were goods sidings on the down side and the goods shed, which never had track in to it, survives as an office and builder's (Tredans) store. The coal yard had been used by a

Merrylands Hotel from the sales particulars in 1913.

40

number of coal merchants, Ranger, Wales, Fred Weale, the Co-op and Hutchinson. There used to be a signal box on the down platform just beyond the station master's house. Electrification of the railway was carried out in 1925. There was a considerable goods and parcel service at the station such that in 1935 the Ratepayers Association asked for a phone to be installed at the station so that enquiries could be made by the public regarding the service. A phone was installed in 1938.

With the coming of the railway Mrs Chrystie engaged Andrew West to build a large temperance hotel in 1885 opposite the station calling it Merrylands Hotel. The hotel had 21 bedrooms, 2 bathrooms and dining accommodation for 200 people. In separate tea houses they could cater for 1,000 children and 300 adults. There was also stabling for 10 horses as well as 3 double coach houses. The hotel had been built on part of Lonesome Farm. During the summer months Mrs Chrystie would invite people from the east end of London to the hotel grounds where they had tea and enjoyed the swings, roundabouts, donkey rides and the bric-a-brac stall. They would also enjoy walking on the common.

With the death of Mrs Chrystie in 1911, the hotel was for sale. In 1917 the owner of the Atlas Works in Little Bookham Street, Thomas Gillett, in partnership with Mr Waring of Waring and Gillow converted the hotel building into offices and built a factory in the hotel grounds which was known as the New Atlas Works. After the war they continued to manufacture engines for aircraft, motor cars and motor cycles and the company had become Gillett, Stephens. Burney and Blackburne also operated in the works. During the Second World War government contracts for war products were undertaken again. After the war the factory became known as the Gillett Works and was used by Wildt Mellor Bromley, a part of the Bentley Engineering Group. They manufactured hosiery making machines and hydraulic equipment, including undercarriages for Hawker aircraft. This ended in 1987 when the old hotel building was demolished and the present office block built in its place for Photo-Me International. The 1917 factory survives and it is now used for the manufacture and servicing of self operating photo booths. The adjoining Bookham Industrial Park was opened at about the same time.

Bookham had been without a blacksmith for a very long time, but in 1975 a blacksmith came to Bookham specialising not in the shoeing of horses but in the manufacture of ornamental and agricultural metal work. Mr Pillow, the blacksmith, bought the ground where he and his family live and work adjacent to the goods yard and, during the construction of his house and adjoining workshop that he has named Boscombe Forge, he found the remains of a railway turntable.

Beyond the station Merrylands Road is on the left. Until the 1950s this was a short road with only 5 or 6 houses and in one of these Andrew West, the builder, lived in his early days in Bookham. Mrs Chrystie had Merryland Cottages built to house the staff from her hotel.

Continuing westwards along Church Road, where the road bends to the left, is the railway bridge to Bookham Grange Hotel. Earlier this had been Burroughs or Burrowes Farm until 1868 when it was up for sale, described in the sale particulars as:

A small pleasure farm, 14 acres of extremely fertile arable, orchard and meadow land with extensive valuable common rights attached. This small but very desirable and freehold estate is situated on the central range of Surrey hills intervening between Leatherhead and Guildford, a most salubrious district with excellent roads and many local advantages.

The farmhouse was developed into a private house named Bayfield. In the 1920s it was unoccupied but in the 1930s it became a nursing home but because it was found to be conducting illegal operations on the premises, it was closed. During World War II, the building was occupied by the Imperial Bank of India that had been evacuated from London. During the 1950s it became the Bookham Grange Hotel as it remained for the rest of the century.

CHAPTER 4

Little Bookham Street

On the west side of the road is Maddox Farm, which has a large black barn fronting the property to the left of the entrance. The original farmhouse was built in the mid-17th century and takes its name from Sir Benjamin Maddox who once owned a considerable amount of property in this area as well as in London where Maddox Street is also named after him. The house has been restored and carefully modernised, but it is the middle part that is the oldest part with low, oak-beamed ceilings, with a height in some cases of less than six feet. The fine old barns are early 18th century and in excellent condition, one has the date 1738 carved on a beam. Although this property has been known as Maddox Farm throughout the 20th century, it had earlier been known as Petty's Farm. It is some seventy years since the place was worked as a farm on an extensive scale when it occupied about 80 acres. Since 1918 many repairs and improvements have been carried out to the house, including the building of a fine oak staircase where previously there was just a ladder to the upper storey. The farm-yard was formed by the house on one side and the barns and other outbuildings flanking the other two sides. This area has now been laid out as a garden immediately in front of the house, while between the barns and the outbuildings are gravel paths and lawns allowing an unobstructed view of the whole setting. In the 1920s and 1930s the house was occupied by Mr Leigh Hutchinson who was a Boy Scout District Commissioner. It is now occupied by Dr Witchalls and his family who came here after working with Albert Schweitzer in Africa.

Further south on the left is what was until a few years ago Wales timber yard. This family operated a sawmill here since the 1880s.

Probably the largest of the West-built houses was that originally named Inglewood in Maddox Lane. It stood in grounds extending to Burnhams Road to the south and Maddox Lane to the west. By 1914 it had been renamed West Hill and was later given the name Foxmead. That name may have been associated with Foxglove Cottage nearby in Little Bookham Street and the neighbouring Fox ale house that was closed by Mrs Chrystie. It is ironic that a Mr Fox lived at the house in the 1930s, however the name Foxmead remained with the house until 1956. Mrs Chrystie had owned the house and when it was sold in 1912 the accommodation included 10 bedrooms, nursery, servants' hall, library, a wide range of reception rooms and a ballroom of considerable size. Miss Jose and her sister came to live here in 1950 after they had sold the Spinney School. After six years they moved to the Priory Coachhouse in Leatherhead and the house was divided into two.

A little further on in Maddox Lane is Maddox Park where from 1939 until the 1960s Mr Sikorska and his wife, who were refugees from Poland, lived. To the rear of the house he built a small canned food factory. After his death his widow continued to live there until in the 1970s the factory was demolished and houses built on the site.

On the opposite side of the Little Bookham Street is the picturesque scene created by Foxglove Cottage, a 16th century house with a brook running through the grounds. The garden on the western side was originally acquired by the ancient rites of squatting and enclosure.

On the south west corner of Little Bookham Street and Burnhams Road is the Village Hall built by Mrs Chrystie in 1902.

Brook Cottage, Little Bookham Street in 1930. The site of the present Village Hall.

44

It stands where Brook Cottages used to be, behind which was Pleasance Row, formerly the Fox ale house, another victim of Mrs Chrystie's temperance beliefs. During World War II meat pies where made and sold in the Village Hall and continued to be so until about 1947. Also during the war ice cream was available here once a month when it was brought to the station in an insulated container.

In the early 1900s Thomas Gillett opened an engineering works, the Atlas Works, in Little Bookham Street. War equipment was made here in both world wars and between the wars they made engines and other parts as well as at the New Atlas Works in Church Road. In 1947 Bookham Engineering Company took over the Old Atlas Works where they carried out servicing to tractors and stationary engines and later steelwork fabrication. They moved to Leatherhead in 1967, the works was demolished in 1968 and the Blackburn flats built on the site.

On the opposite side of the road is the site of Gastons, a large Victorian house that had stood well back from the road and was approached via a long curved drive with an entrance in both Little Bookham Street and Sole Farm Road. I understand that the house was built of Swedish timber and then bricked over. Earlier it had been Gastons Farm which extended northwards from Sole Farm Road. Gastons was occupied by Mr Kirkpatrick, a retired head-master of Lurgan College, and his wife from 1913 until his death, however Mrs Kirkpatrick continued to live there until at least 1927. Clive Lewis (C S Lewis) spent two and a half years with the Kirkpatricks at the Gastons from 1914 before he joined the army and later became a scholar of English Mediaeval and Renaissance literature. Lewis died in 1963 and is best remembered for his children's books and his books on Christianity. The house was demolished in 1965 when more houses were built on the site, a part of the original drive and an outhouse still remain.

A little further along on the west side of Little Bookham Street is Grape Vine Cottage or, as it used to be known, Vine Cottage. This 16th century house originally had no chimneys and smoke would have come out of openings at the apex of the roof. John William Elston, a boot and shoe repairer, lived and worked at Grape Vine Cottage from around 1909 until about 1950.

Weale's shop is nearby. In 1902 Mrs Mary Ann Weale moved to no 111, which is next door to the present shop at no 113. In 1912 her son, Frank Weale, started a coal business in the neighbouring yard with an office at no 107; he later sold coke and paraffin as well as coal. Next to the coal yard was the farm where they kept cows, pigs, chickens etc until after World War II. The farm buildings were demolished in 1997 and houses built on the site. A general store was opened at no 109 with the post office being added around 1914. Later the shop was transferred to no 111; a further move came much later with an expansion of the business when the shop was transferred to no 113, with the addition of a considerable extension, as it was in1999. From 1923 until at least 1928 Frank Weale was Overseer for the Parish of Little Bookham. He married a cousin of Andrew West, the builder, and their son Howard married Vera who continued to run the business after Howard's death until she retired in the early 1990s.

In the 1950s and 1960s there was a Romany caravan among the farm buildings. Mr Harris lived here repairing pots and pans and china goods for a living. After Weales had moved from no 109 the shop was occupied by Mr Fitzgerald, a boot and shoe repairer, until about 1970. He was a very active member of the Bookham Baptist Church and an officer in the Boys' Brigade.

Near the junction of Sole Farm Road and Little Bookham Street there had been a girls' private school in the early part of the century. It was named Woodfield and the headmistress was Miss Smith.

Just into Sole Farm Road are three modern bungalows. These were built on the site of a corrugated iron bungalow which had been occupied by Mrs Ragget for a very long time. It was bought and demolished in the 1970s.

Continuing along Little Bookham Street, on the east side, is Whitehouse Cottage. This was until recently two cottages in a row of three which were probably built in the 16th century. Its present owner, Mr Whitehouse, has carried out an immense amount of restoration on the cottage almost entirely on his own.

Among a number of other cottages in this part of Little Bookham built around the beginning of the century are Shaftesbury Cottages built in 1899 by Alfred Wales. These are distinguishable by the inlay of stone coloured bricks running in a line around the walls. Two of the cottages have been occupied by members of the Wales family since they were built and continue to be the homes of a grand daughter and a great grand daughter of the builder. There was a house next door to the Shaftesbury Cottages which was demolished when the present shop was built. The shop was occupied by F Sayers, baker and grocer, from the mid 1930s until the 1970s and it has since been occupied by Paws and Claws selling animal food.

On the other side of the road there are a number of semi-detached houses that were built by the Epsom Urban District Council in the late 1920s. Next door to these houses was Bennetts Cafe which closed in the 1960s.

On the east side of Little Bookham Street, behind a row of tall cupressus trees, is the picturesque 17th century Pound Cottage. Next door to Pound Cottage are two semi-detached houses that, although much smaller than the Andrew West houses we have already met, were built by him. West himself had moved from Merrylands Road to Milton Villas in Little Bookham Street, two semi-detached houses that he built and owned in 1900.

Next is a small housing development built in recent years called Bennetts Farm Place, the name being taken from the Bennetts Farm that occupied this site in the 19th century. In 1913 the farm buildings and the yard were occupied by Norris and Company, which was a small building firm. In 1920 Andrew West set up a builders yard and workshops on the Bennetts Farm site and he lived in the neighbouring house, Springfield, which was probably built by his company. The family connection ceased in 1968 with the sale of the firm and the last relative to live at Springfield was Mrs James West who moved out in 1971. The site was sold in the 1980s but in 1989 the workshop buildings were burnt down. In 1992 Springfield was also demolished and the development called Bennetts Farm Place was built.

Half Moon Cottage is on the north east corner of Little Bookham Street and Lower Road and it is one of the oldest properties in the area. Earlier Half Moon Cottage had been one of a number of ale houses in Bookham that were closed by Mrs Chrystie. Between 1909 and the 1920s it was owned by Arthur Bird. When I visited the cottage I could see from the brickwork that a number of alterations had taken place including the addition of a chimney on the north east corner of the building. Here was a 16th century cottage where the walls leaned, the ceilings sagged, the floors sloped, the windows hung at various angles and the neat little staircase was positively dangerous. In one of the living rooms the original fireplace, which appears to have been completely untouched, opens out to about eight feet wide. I have been told by several people that during World War II a man known as the King of Poland lived at the cottage. He was believed to have been an eccentric Polish count, but that may have been due to the fact that he wore what was considered to be traditional Polish dress.

John Harvey lived at Half Moon Cottage from the 1950s until 1975. He had been educated at St. John's, Leatherhead and later studied architecture. A conscientious objector at the outbreak of the war he was employed by the Ministry of Public Works in helping to preserve bomb damaged buildings. Later still, he specialised in historical architecture, writing many books on the subject. Among the many positions that he held, Harvey was President of the Garden History Society and served for thirty years on the Council for Ancient Monuments Society. He wrote an account of Bookham's history between the 13th and 19th centuries that was published in the Bookhams Bulletin in serial form, starting with part 1 in March 1953 and ending with part 24 in December 1959. He married in 1934 and one of his two sons continued to live at Half Moon Cottage until 1999. John Harvey died in 1997, aged 86, at Frome in Somerset.

Now to return to the Windsor Castle public house on the other side of the road. This has its origins in the 16th century and was previously known as the Castle Inn. In the later part of the 19th century a member of the Weale family was the landlord and at that time one could buy groceries, coal and coke here as well as alcoholic drinks. After Mr Weale's death in 1902 his widow was fined for allowing drunkenness on one occasion when she and her son left the pub and opened the store further down Little Bookham Street. Until 1923 the inn had been owned by the Cobham Brewery but this was taken over by the brewers Watney Coombe and Reid. In the late 1960s and early 1970s the landlord was Mr C V Bookham.

Next door to the Windsor Castle is Rose Cottage which was probably built in the 18th century as there are bricks marked with I M 1746, probably the builder's initials and the date of construc-

Ye Olde Windsor Castle in the early 1930s.

tion. Originally it was a small detached cottage that was extended around the year 1850 converting it into two semi-detached cottages, and evidence of this may be seen both inside and outside. Later still the two cottages were amalgamated into one and the rear single storey extension added. Mr Cattermole, the present owner has carried out much renovation to the house over the last few years. Close by are two semi-detached cottages built in 1881 as part of Preston Farm. Both houses have been extended in the last twenty years. The Post House, the front part of which is of the 18th century and of brick and timber was a Post House before the post office was introduced to Weale's shop. Next door is The Old School House which was the National School from the 1880s.

Dawes Cottage, a half-timbered 16th century building, was originally two houses. In 1974 this house was in a very poor state but it was then occupied by Dr Witchalls, now of Maddox Farm, who carried out extensive restoration. During the course of renovation an inglenook fireplace was uncovered in each of the two living rooms. In the case of one of them four other fireplaces had been concealed each one in front of another. To one side of the second inglenook fireplace was a bread oven which also had been concealed. A sealed cellar was discovered beneath the house and it was used to increase the headroom in the ground floor rooms.

CHAPTER 5

Lower Road

Turning right at the crossroads Preston Farm Cottages are on the right. These two semi-detached houses were built in 1905 by Andrew West to house the workers from Preston Farm. Reg Williams was born in one of them and Vera Weale was born in the other, each of whom has helped me with the book.

In Manor House Lane is Manor House School in the old manor house entered through the large hall, with its spacious, impressive staircase and first floor open landing. This is the oldest part of the building, dating from the early 18th century which had been the home of the Lords of the Manor of Little Bookham. Henry Court Willock became Lord of the Manor in 1906 and, adopting the family name of Pollen, he changed his surname to Willock-Pollen. Lack of funds obliged the Pollen family at various times to live either at the Old Rectory or Manor Farm, while letting out the Manor House. In 1914 Little Bookham Manor, The Rectory and The Grange occupied 30 acres. Mrs Willock-Pollen encouraged the game of stoolball to be played and in one game at Preston Cross in 1912 a ladies team played the Effingham cricket team but the men had the handicap of playing with the right hand in their trousers pocket and the ladies won.

In 1927 a fire almost gutted the Manor House but fortunately the building was saved and restored. After Willock-Pollen's death in 1934 the estate was broken up; the Manor House and the Lordship were acquired in 1936 by Miss H E Green who ran a school in Mickleham. She brought her school here and it became known as Manor House School. It has continued to expand over the years with many new buildings in the grounds. On her retirement Miss Green moved to a timbered house in the school grounds, until she died in the early 1960s.

In the school grounds there is a barn from Preston House garden which had been used for storing store fruit and vegetables. The barn was damaged by gales in October 1987 and in 1990.

Manor House Little Bookham after the fire in 1927.

Urgent action was needed to save it and in October 1990 the barn was dismantled and transferred to the school where it was reassembled and repaired by volunteers from the Leatherhead and District Countryside Protection Society and the Local History Society. The 150–200 year old barn rests on 9 staddle stones and is similar to the one at Maddox Farm described earlier. It is now used by the school for storage purposes.

On the opposite side of Manor House Lane was Manor Farm, an active dairy farm until around the 1950s. Among the farm buildings which remain there is a very long 15th century tithe barn in excellent condition.

Returning to Lower Road on the left is a cast-iron electricity distribution cabinet. Printed on the door is *London and Home Counties Joint Electricity Authority, Electric House, Leatherhead*. This authority took over the electricity supply to Leatherhead in 1930.

Not far away is Little Bookham Church. This dates from the 12th century and has a register dating from 1651. The building is of stone and rubble with a wooden turret containing one bell. In 1901 the church was enlarged by the addition of an organ chamber on the north side of the chancel. Excavations at the churchyard in 1951 revealed many pieces of early pottery, tiles, a knife blade and a small boar's tusk. In the churchyard west of the church is a yew tree that is considered to be 700 years old.

Returning to Lower Road is Elmhurst, a double fronted house that still retains its Edwardian ornate ridge tiles. Next there are the buildings of Preston Farm which was run by Mr Roberts from the 1930s until the 1950s when he had 40 head of cattle. Since the farm closed the buildings have been used for a number of industrial activities. On the opposite side of the road there is a small building with a tapered roof at one end giving it the appearance of an oasthouse which was used for pig food preparation.

Turning right into Rectory Lane, Preston Cross Hotel is on the right. This was a private house known as Preston House and owned by the Lord of the Manor. Earlier it had housed a boys' boarding school but from 1919 until the 1950s it was occupied by the Hansard family. During World War II Mrs Hansard, then a widow, lived alone in the house with two schoolboy evacuees. The boys lived in the servants quarters while Mrs Hansard occupied the main house where she dined alone but always dressed for dinner. On Sundays the boys were taken by Mrs Hansard to Little Bookham Church in the Daimler dressed in their Sunday best. One of them is quoted as saying 'Here we enjoyed the hospitality of a kind elderly lady who, in trying to unite our family, provided us with a rare insight into the formal luxury of a lifestyle now long gone. After church on Sundays we would troop around the house ceremoniously winding the clocks.' The last private occupant of Preston House was Mr Thompson, an eye specialist, who kept about a hundred pigs in the field to the rear of the premises. The kiln-like building in Lower Road was where the pig food was prepared and Mr Thompson had the kiln built for this purpose. He and the pig farm were there until the late 1960s. The Preston Cross Hotel opened in about 1970.

Further along Rectory Lane is the Grange Training Centre and Workshop for the Disabled. An Elizabethan style cottage here was bought by Alfred Bird in 1897 and enlarged to something approaching what it is today. It was described as being all that a gentleman could wish for but it was not so large that it would present a problem at a time when servants were generally becoming more difficult to hire. The accommodation included two large drawing rooms and a large dining room, a morning room and a study, as well as a range of domestic premises with back hall and staircase. Bird also altered the course of Rectory Lane from being directly in front of the house to where the road is today, at the same time he arranged for the parish boundary to be moved westwards so that The Grange was no longer within the Little Bookham parish but in the parish of Great Bookham. Sometime after his wife's death he married the family's nurse who, after his death, in 1931, had a house built on the corner of Rectory Lane and Lower Road named Orchard Grange.

In 1938 the School of Stitchery and Lace came to The Grange. They trained disabled people in needlework skills as well as providing sheltered workshops and accommodation. It is now the Grange Training Centre for the Disabled but the aim is still to encourage maximum independence and personal fulfilment through the mastery of a variety of skills.

Further along the lane is the 18th century house that had been the Rectory until 1900. During World War II Queen Marie of Yugoslavia, who was a war refugee, occupied the house. Two military policemen maintained guard outside the house throughout the war years and until 1947 when she moved. Then Sam Eckman, an American representative of Metro-Goldwyn-Meyer, lived in the house until 1958 since when the property has fallen into a state of neglect and most of the furnishings and fittings have been removed.

Orchard Grange, built for Mrs Bird, is on the corner of Rectory Lane and Lower Road. It was occupied in the 1950s by Mr Cross, an amateur film maker, who had a film studio built alongside the house, which still stands today. Reg Williams, who had served on local farms all of his working life, acted the major role in a film made by Mr Cross that illustrated the rural way of life in Bookham at the time.

Turning right towards Great Bookham there is a new small development of three properties on the left. Until around the 1970s, this plot had been occupied by a smithy since the latter part of the 19th century. This was held by three generations of the Hamshar family; Edward, Thomas and Percy who lived at the 16th century Halfway House that is on the corner of Lower Road and Childs Hall Road. Earlier the house had been divided into two with Edward Hamshar and his family occupying the left hand or west side of the house and the right hand or east side was used by a man named Stedman where he ran his building business. Early in the 20th century David McFarlane ran a dairy in the right hand part before he moved to Phoenice Farm in Dorking Road. The dairy here was taken over by Albert Farrow in 1911 until he moved to the High Street, near The Royal Oak, in 1916.

Towards the end of the 19th century Edward Hamshar opened an ale house in his part of the house; he died in 1893 and his son, Thomas took over the blacksmith's business. After the death of Edward's widow in 1902 Mrs Chrystie bought the property and closed the ale house. In the 1930s the blacksmith's business passed to Thomas's son Percy but as the demand for the shoeing of horses diminished the business ended as a knife grinding service until the 1970s. A contemporary advertisement stated *T. Hamshar, Engineer and Smith, Hot and Cold Water Engineer and All Kinds of Iron Work*. The entrance to Halfway House was originally at the front but it is now in Childs Hall Road. The oldest part of the house is the northern part which dates from the 16th or 17th century and is brick and half-timbered with later extensions. There is a double pitched roof and there is a drop in floor levels between the front and back of the house, possibly because it was originally two houses.

On the opposite corner of Childs Hall Road is a house named Childs, the original, eastern, part of which dates from the 16th or 17th century. This was Bugg's Farm, occupying 10 acres, until at least 1926 and was owned by The Oaken Wood Co. Ltd, but in more recent times, it became known as Childs Haugh. Just to the east of Childs on the opposite side of Lower Road there is an underground spring known as the Earborne which flooded the road every few years. In 1947 this flowed for two weeks and on many occasions buses have had to be diverted when the road was flooded.

Moving towards the centre of the village there are some post-war houses built on fields on which Preston Farm grazed cattle. The next houses date from the mid 1930s and were built by Metcalfe similar to some he built in Little Bookham Street. Middlemead estate was built by Leatherhead Urban District Council in the early 1960s. At about the same time The Garstons and the surrounding private development took place.

On the corner of the Garstons and Lower Road is the site of Church House that was built for the parish church in 1928. It was opened by the Queen Mother when she was Duchess of York. It was demolished in 1978 to make way for the present flats, known as Church House, that were built on the site. Since the Hall was paid for by local public subscriptions extreme disappointment was voiced when it was known that the public was to have no say in the future of the hall. The building had all the functions of a church hall; jumble sales, wedding receptions, dances, whist drives, concerts etc. In 1935 it cost £2–2–0. per night to hire, with 'good lighting, ventilation and central heating provided'. The hall was used as a First Aid Post during the war years when it was surrounded by a wall of sandbags. In 1947 the Leatherhead Urban District Council set up the Bookham Pie Centre at the Hall where meat pies were made and sold, to assist families with their meat ration.

On the south side of Lower Road until about 1950 was a large field that embraced what is now, the recreation ground, The Lorne and adjacent houses. The field was known as 'Madge's Field' as Mr Madge, the butcher, used it for growing crops. In the 1950s and 1960s the development of Lower Road, The Lorne, Glebe Close, Swann's Meadow, Hawkwood Rise and Hawkwood Dell took place. At the junction of Hawkwood Rise and Guildford Road stands Hawkwood House. This was built at the beginning of the 20th century and Mrs Swann occupied it from 1904 until the early 1920s when the Westondarp family moved there until around 1940; until 1925 the house was called Ballinveny. In the 1950s the house was divided into apartments at the same time as the grounds were developed for housing. One of the residents of Hawkwood House is Mr Winterson whose father was station master at Bookham from 1916 until 1932 and he went to school at St James and was a choir boy at St Nicolas Church.

Turning left on Guildford Road there are two blocks of flats called Yelverton Court. They were named after Admiral Yelverton, a retired gentleman who lived in Mead House until his death in 1959 aged 96. He is remembered as a gentleman who often walked down the High Street wearing a brown trilby hat, a tweed overcoat and highly polished brown shoes. He bade everyone that he passed the time of day, always raising his hat to the ladies. Mead House was demolished in 1962 and Yelverton Court built on the site. Mr Pickering-Pick, who earlier was on the committees of the village silver band and the Barn Hall, lived at Grove Farm Cottage next door to Mead House.

White's Garage on Lower Road was built in the early 1920s for Mr Armstrong who had it until the mid 1930s. He called it simply, the Bookham Garage but it has been extended several times and had several names. In the 1970s it was owned by Ken Barrington, the county and test cricketer.

On the other side of Lower Road is the Scout Hut built in the 1930s with a later hall adjacent to it. Broseley Cottages are a row of semi-detached houses built in 1904 which were owned by the Davis family of The Mill in Church Road.

Just opposite in Lower Road is Rose Cottage, another 16th century survivor. Also on this side of Lower Road is Slinfold Cottage, another 16th century property. At the turn of the century this was the home of Mr Simpson who was a blacksmith, who also sold, hired and repaired bicycles and stabled horses in the adjacent buildings. The business continued into the 1930s under various names.

Townshott Close (which was named School Lane until about 1913) follows the route of an ancient road that continued southwards across Guildford Road, to what is now White Way. The school and the headmaster's house were given by the Dawnay family in 1856. Originally the school consisted of one large room in which boys sat on one side and girls on the other but it was extended in 1910 when the school in Eastwick Road was closed.

An idea of school life at the time may be gained from these extracts from the school log:–

Absenteeism from school was often excused because of the lack of boots or shoes; A very dirty neglected child that lived in a tent on the Common came to school, whose family was removed to the workhouse; In February 1895, the weather was extremely cold, such that the ink in the inkwells froze; Mrs Chrystie, Miss Dyer and other ladies in the Parish gave 24 of the poorest boys dinner at the Coffee Tavern every day this week

William Charles Vellender had been schoolmaster at Bookham School since 1890 and remained so until his sudden death in 1913 after becoming ill while taking a class. He was succeeded by Henry Francis Griffin who remained at the school until the mid 1930s. He has been reported as being an extremely good headmaster, strict but kind and respected by the children. Mr Griffin was followed by Mr Richards who was headmaster for 20 years retiring in 1951 and was replaced by Arthur Browning.

The school had been a church school until it was taken over by the Surrey County Council following the Education Act of 1902 when it then became an Elementary School. In 1982 the school moved to its present site and was renamed the Dawnay School. The library that had been at Lower Shott for 30 years, housed in the stable buildings of Bookham Grove, was moved into part of the school building in December 1988. The remainder of the school building was converted for residential use.

Bookham Baptist Church is on the corner of Townshott Close and Lower Road. The original, eastern, part was built in 1911 in memory of Mrs Chrystie and called the Peace Memorial Hall. This provided all the usual functions of a village hall with billiards, weddings and whist drives, etc. Mrs Swann of Hawkwood House had raised the mortgage for the building of the hall but at her death the Hall was still in debt. George Cook of Sole Farm House, a Baptist lay preacher and organiser of the Boys Brigade, hired the hall for Sunday evening services from 1925 until he acquired

The Crown from Lower Road looking towards Fetcham in the late 1920s. Note the Wall's ice cream tricycle outside Steven's shop.

the hall and it became the Baptist Church in the early 1930s. Later the hall and Sunday school buildings were added to the right of the church.

Past The Crown is East Street. At the corner there was an air raid siren on a metal post which remained in place until the 1970s. There had been a horse trough here but this was removed before World War II. East Street was known as Back Lane until around 1906.

The first house on the right is Graham Lodge which was built before 1914. Harold Bostock lived here from 1918 until he moved to Fife Lodge, Church Road, probably in 1922. Until the early 1940s Alan Fenn lived at Graham Lodge. He had been a racing motorist who raced at the Isle of Man before the motor cycle T T races began.

Next door are two semi-detached modern houses which were built on the site of Victoria Hall. The hall was the village hall which had been built for Mrs Chrystie on the site of a house called Toppetts. It was made largely of corrugated iron and was known as 'The Tabernacle' or 'The Iron Room'. Mrs Chrystie held her temperance meetings in the hall which had a stage, gallery and seating for about 200. At the rear there were two large recreation rooms, a store and a miniature rifle range. A solid fuel stove was the only source of heating for the hall. Oliver Goldsmith, of Church Road, ran a club in the hall for young men and boys where table-tennis, pool, bagatelle, and other games were played. Mrs Chrystie was a great supporter of the village silver band which rehearsed and played in the Victoria Hall in the early part of the century until 1914, and then in the 1930s. The band used to play

Victoria Hall, East Street in 1950.

on the lawns of the big houses such as The Grove, Eastwick Park, Ballenvenny and The Gables during the summer months for dancing. Dances were also held at the Recreation Ground, admission 3d. Although attempts were made after World War II to resurrect the band it was not until 1973 that it was re-formed. The Temperance Club met in the hall, no doubt with Mrs Chrystie's blessing, and there was a nigger minstrel troupe composed of members of the local football and cricket clubs that gave concerts with Mr Bates, the postmaster, as the regular 'comic'. The Working Men's Club used the hall until they moved to the Old Barn Hall. In 1905 Mrs Chrystie sold the hall to Richard Lee who retained it until the mid 1920s.

The Victoria Hall was not used publicly after World War I and with disuse its condition deteriorated. In 1924, with the acute shortage of living accommodation, two families were moved into the Hall, one occupied the theatre while the other lived in the recreation rooms. There was no washing or drinking water available in the building and water was drawn from an outside tap in nearby Stents Alley. George White, who lived here as a boy, recalled in some detail the operation in which his tonsils were removed by Dr Ede on the kitchen table under only a local anaesthetic. He also recalls taking the rent for his mother for the accommodation in the Victoria Hall to Mr Lee at his office in The High

Street. Happily, in 1928, the two families were transferred to the newly built council houses nearby, known as Fairfield Cottages.

The Victoria Hall was used in the early 1930s by Shepherd and Rogers, fruiterer and greengrocer. In the 1950s and 60s, Reynolds Furnishings used it for furniture repairs and Bookham Granaries used it as a store. The hall was finally demolished in 1975 and the present houses were built in its place.

Further along East Street there is a small bungalow called The Woolpack which may date from the 16th century and was a store for a farm in the High Street. At the time of the First World War it was used as an office by Richard Lee the architect. It has been residential for at least 60 years and many alterations and improvements have been carried out to the property.

Moving further south no 8 used to have a large window and door at the front. This presumably had been a butcher's shop and evidence can still be seen where a steel bar was fixed for hanging meat. This is the only house in East Street to have a cellar. Arthur Sayer had a shop in East Street until 1905 when he moved to the cross roads and his shop in East Street was occupied by Mellor until Harry Edser took it over until at least 1925. The property remains in private occupation with the front door moved to the side of the house.

A more recent but startling piece of history occurred early one

Gas explosion in East Street in 1986.

morning at Stoneleigh, no 1 Fairfield Terrace which is owned and occupied by Mr and Mrs Kemp. On the morning of 5th March 1986 Mrs Kemp and her son were upstairs whilst Mr Kemp was in the kitchen having put the kettle on. He became aware of a strong smell of gas and immediately phoned British Gas who told him to turn off the supply at the main. He had just done this and opened the windows when there was an enormous explosion that removed the front and most of the upper floor of the house. Fire then followed the explosion and the street was sealed off and neighbours were evacuated from their homes as gas engineers desperately tried to find the source of the leak. Mr Kemp had his face and hands very badly burned, Mrs Kemp, physically unhurt, managed to jump down from what was left of the landing to the ground and their son was blown to the opposite side of the road but miraculously he also was unhurt. After treatment in Epsom Hospital for burns and shock they returned to Bookham later that afternoon to stay with relatives. Two cars were crushed by falling masonry. Firemen from four stations fought the blaze and had it under control in less than an hour. Some residents had to stay away from their homes until late afternoon when all danger from gas had gone and the houses had been well ventilated. A fractured gas main outside the front of the house was believed to be the cause of the explosion. The road was cleared by early evening. Eventually the house was replaced by two houses of a similar style to the original property.

Walking back down East Street towards Lower Road, on the right hand side are the houses that are part of the estate built in the 1920s by the Epsom Urban District Council. Between these houses and the later houses on this side there is a path which leads to Eastwick Road and this path is the route of the original 3 inch main laid in the 1880s to bring gas from Leatherhead to Bookham. The remaining houses in the street were built in what was the garden of The Hermitage in Lower Road and many will remember the whole plot north of the path being surrounded by a corrugated iron fence.

The Hermitage was known as Fairfield until 1913, when the name Fairfield was transferred to the large house in the High Street. The Hermitage is of the 18th century when it was a much smaller property but it has been added to and altered over the years, including the raising of the low ceilings by two or three feet. In 1792 the novelist Fanny Burney met Alexandre d'Arblay, one of the French émigrés living at Juniper Hall, and they married in the following year and lived for a short time at Phoenice Farm before moving to Fairfield later in the year. Here she bore her only child, who was christened in Bookham Church. By this time she had already written 'Evelina' and 'Cecilia' which had been published anonymously since it was not the done thing for young ladies to write novels. The books had been widely admired by many influential people, including Dr Johnson and his circle, who were amazed when it was revealed that the author was a woman. The novel 'Camilla' was written here and from the proceeds she was able to build Camilla Cottage at Westhumble. Surgeon Major Frederic Stedman lived at Fairfield in the late 1800s and his widow continued to live there after his death

The Emuss family occupied the house at the turn of the 19th century and in 1904 Sir William and Lady Blanche Bousfield moved into Fairfield. Sir William died in 1914 but Lady Bousfield, who was said to be something of a recluse, continued to live there until at least 1935. A second generation of the Emuss family then lived here from the mid 1930s until the 1970s. At the apex of the roof of the house there is a bell which used to be used to call the workers in from the neighbouring hopfields and the stable block at the front of the house has a crane which was used to lift hay into the store on the first floor. During World War II there was a concrete pillbox in the west corner of the front garden. Quite recently the stable block was converted into a workshop when the roof was raised a couple of feet.

Next door is Hop Garden Cottage. The name is derived from when hops were grown in the fields at the rear of the house as far as Leatherhead Road. When the hops were no longer grown there corn was grown each year until Keswick's death in 1912 when the land was sold. Mr Chitty, who was a boot maker and also the Overseer of the Parish of Great Bookham, lived with his family at Hop Garden Cottage from the early 1900s until 1918, when another well-known Bookham family named Miller moved into cottage. In the single-storey, lean-to brick building to the right of the cottage Walter Wood ran his boot and shoe repair business after he moved from Church Road and remained here until the late 1940s when he moved to Guildford Road, where he carried on for about another ten years.

House building on the south side of Lower Road between Hop Garden Cottage and Eastwick Road was piecemeal through the 1920s and 1930s. There were two bungalows, almost opposite Eastwick Park Avenue, that were built by Mr Scarlett. One of these, no 175, remains. The second bungalow, no 173, was Roadside Cottage where Dr Ede had his practice from 1922 until

1935. When a young newly-qualified Dr Easton took over the practice in 1935 he had the bungalow converted to the large house that stands today. The north west part of the ground floor can still be identified as part of the original Scarlett bungalow. Dr Easton, a physician and surgeon, quickly gained the confidence of his patients and built up a wonderful reputation as their general practitioner. He was also a police surgeon. I have been told a number of stories of his willingness and readiness to answer calls and attend his patients, particularly during air raids throughout World War II. In 1971 he moved house and practise to The Tyrrells in Church Road where sadly he died in 1991.

The bungalows on the north side of Lower Road were also built in the early 1920s by Mr Scarlett after the Eastwick Park Estate had been fragmented and sold off. The front gardens of these bungalows were shortened at the front in the 1960s to enable the road to be widened. In 1982–3 one of those bungalows was demolished to enable Pine Walk to be built; this is an example of the infilling which has taken place over the last few decades in the village.

CHAPTER 6

Eastwick Park

The gates to the bungalow at no 182a, Lower Road are the original gates of Eastwick Park, one for vehicles and a small gate either side for pedestrians. The drive used to curve round to the right towards the front of the house through beautifully landscaped grounds with various specimen trees. In 1806 Eastwick Park stood in 380 acres with a frontage on Lower Road from St Nicolas Church to just beyond Eastwick Drive. By 1914 the estate had been reduced to 150 acres. The house was one of the first in Bookham to have electric lighting powered by batteries that were charged by a gas engine-driven dynamo until around 1935. William Keswick of Eastwick Park was Member of Parliament for Epsom and the last traditional Lord of the Manor of Great Bookham. He and his family resided at Eastwick Park from 1882 with a staff of nine plus a nanny and a maid. Before Keswick it was occupied by David Barclay of the Barclay Perkins brewery company who lived with his wife and only child at Eastwick, cared for by a staff of 16 servants. Keswick's first wife Amelia Sophie had died in 1883, aged 36, but some years later he remarried to Alice Henrietta who was born in Dublin. Some years after Keswick's death she remarried and lived until 1966 aged 93. Keswick died in 1912, aged 78, and is buried in St. Nicolas' churchyard. His son, Henry, sold the house and manor in 1918 to a retired sugar planter named Souchon, who wanted to cash in on the timber shortage after the war. Public objection to the felling of the trees persuaded Souchon to sell the property and in 1922 a property developer and estate agent, Percy Portway Harvey, bought the Eastwick Estate and began the disintegration of the estate. In 1924 Harvey agreed to the closing of the level crossing that used to be at the north end of what is now Eastwick Drive and in return the London and South Western Railway Company allowed traffic to use the Glade bridge for further development on the north side of the railway. A large part of the estate became available but it was

Particulars, &c.

EASTWICK PARK,

WITH MANOR, CAPITAL MANSION, AND ESTATE,

At Great Bookham,

NEAR LEATHERHEAD, SURREY,

CONSISTS OF

The Manor of Great Bookham,

With its Rights, Members, and Appurtenances.

THE ROYALTIES EXTEND NEARLY OVER THE WHOLE PARISH,

CONSISTING OF ABOUT

2,280 Acres of Cultivated Land,

AND ABOUT

Seven Hundred and Eighty-five Acres of most Fertile and Picturesque Common or Waste Land,

CALLED BOOKHAM AND RANMORE COMMONS:

Bookham Common ....Acres	349	
Ranmore Ditto	436	
(Be the same more or less)	785	

The whole affording great facility for Breeding & Preserving Game

ALSO,

Sundry Quit Rents, Fines on Death or Alienation, Heriots on Death, Court Baron, Court Leet, and other Manorial Rights;

Among which is the Lord's valuable Right to the Growing Timber on Bookham and Ranmore Commons,

ABOUT 400 ACRES

OF WHICH ARE

COVERED WITH FLOURISHING OAK, BEECH, ASH, AND OTHER TIMBER TREES.

The several Quit Rents amount to about £7. per Annum;

All the Copyholds (except one small property, which is held at Fine certain of 10s. on Alienation only) are subject to Fines, at the will of the Lord, on Death or Alienation.

THE ESTIMATED ANNUAL VALUE OF THE COPYHOLDS,

Subject to Fine at will, is about

FIVE HUNDRED POUNDS.

The Fine certain on Alienation of the excepted Copyhold, is 10s.; on Death this Fine is at will.

There are Forty-seven Heriots of the best Beast.

The Lord of the Manor is also entitled to a Third of the Oak Timber felled for Sale on the Copyhold Lands.

Sales particulars for an earlier sale of Eastwick Park

EASTWICK PARK,

With its Mansion, has long been regarded as one of the elegant ornaments of this Picturesque and Delightful part of the County of Surrey.

THE MANSION,

A substantial square Stuccoed Edifice, placed on a moderately elevated Site, and near the Village of Great Bookham, is surrounded on three sides by secluded and richly Timbered Lawns, but commands in one direction

An open Landscape of great Extent and Beauty,

Presents Four several Fronts, in simple good taste, with little Architectural Embellishment,

And contains abundant Accommodation for a Family of Fashion or distinction,

VIZ.—

ON THE GROUND FLOOR,

A Hall, used as a Billiard Room, 27 feet square, entered by Wainscot Folding Doors, Pannelled with Plate Glass;

On the Left of this is

A Library or Morning Room, 25 by 20 feet, with Mahogany Doors, the Chimney Piece of Dove Coloured Marble;

Beyond it, a small Library, with Coved Ceiling, and a Semicular Bow, the Windows to the Floor, that in the centre opening to a Descent by Stone Steps to the Pleasure Grounds;

The Doors of this Room are Pannelled with Plate Glass, the Chimney Piece of Statuary Marble.

Behind this is a Corridor from the Dining Room to the Offices, having a Flight of Steps to the Pleasure Ground, and in it a Store Room, containing a Strong Closet, with Iron Shelves and Door;

And near this a Water Closet.

On the Right of the Hall,

A NOBLE SALOON OR DRAWING ROOM,
71 Feet by 20,

Extending the entire depth of the Mansion,

Having a Statuary Marble Chimney Piece in the Centre, Mahogany Doors, the Centre Windows to the Floor, opening on to a Paved Platform and to the Pleasure Grounds.

This truly elegant Apartment is intersected by Two beautiful Screens of Ionic Columns, of Scagliola, in imitation of Red Breccia; beyond which, to obviate the possibility of Cold in Winter, are Two concealed Stoves, masked by false Armoires or Bookpresses, giving equal Warmth to each extremity of the Saloon.

THE DINING ROOM
Contiguous,

Of singular but most beautiful proportions, is 31 feet by 21 feet, (exclusive of a Recess on one side); with Eliptic Coved Ceiling, entered by a Door, of fine Wainscot, at each end for introducing the Dinner;

The Chimney Piece, of Statuary Marble, is in a Semicircular Recess, with a Niche for a Statue on each side.

The Principal and back Staircases occupy the centre of the Mansion;

The former constructed in a Stone-Paved Inner Hall, is of Oak; wide, and of easy ascent;

The Landing above is surrounded by an Open Arcade on Three sides, from which the Principal Bed Chambers are severally entered;

A false Arcade on the Fourth side conceals the back Stairs.

65

THE PRINCIPAL BED CHAMBER,

Is 25 feet by 20 feet.

Adjoining and communicating therewith, is

A Lady's Morning Room or Dressing Room, with Semicircular Bow, Chimney Piece of Black Marble, the Folding Doors of Entrance on each side Pannelled with Looking Glass.

Five other best Bed Chambers,

Four of them with Dressing Rooms (large enough for Beds,) and having Fireplaces in each.

A Water Closet, Housemaid's Closet, and Sink.

ON THE ATTIC FLOOR,

Are Ten Bachelors' and Servants' Sleeping Rooms.

Water is thrown up to this Upper Floor.

The Roof is most substantially Slated and Leaded.

A Second back Staircase, on the descent of which is another Water Closet, leads to

A WING,

ON THE FIRST FLOOR OF WHICH ARE

A very spacious Housekeeper's Room, Sleeping Room, Store Room, and Still Room, and beyond is a Fruit Chamber.

THE GROUND FLOOR OF THE WING

Is occupied by a spacious Kitchen, a Scullery, ample cool Larders; And beyond these are a Brew House and Malt House.

ON THE BASEMENT,

Are a Servants' Hall, capital Arched Wine and other Cellars, Butler's Pantry, and a Forcing Pump to supply the Upper Part of the Dwelling.

A DETACHED

Brick and Tiled Building, with Two advancing Wings,

CONTAINS

A Dairy, Wash House, and Laundry.

Near which is a Pump of never-failing and fine Water.

A Four-stall and a Three-stall Stable, and a loose Box;

A Double and a Single Coach House, Corn Chamber, and Harness Room.

THE KITCHEN GARDEN contains rather more than TWO ACRES,

Enclosed by a capital Fruit Wall, and abundantly Planted.

External Potageries, in which are a Grapery and a Succession House.

Also, a Drying Yard, with useful Sheds.

A SMALL PLEASURE GROUND SURROUNDS THE HOUSE,

Leading to, and partly concealing, the Offices.

In a Grove, on the skirt of the Park, and not far distant from the Dwelling, are Two small Octagonal Buildings, Brick-built and Thatched; the one

An Ornamental Dairy,

The other a Scalding House, connected by a Thatched Open Corridor;

And near these is an Ice House.

stipulated that it was to be for residential use only and for houses selling at not less than £1000 each with the exception that land adjoining Leatherhead Road was cheaper with small bungalows from £500 upwards.

In the mid-1920s Eastwick Park house and the surrounding land was bought by Mr Fussell who had a boys' preparatory school at Worthing, called Southey Hall, which he moved to Eastwick. Approximately where the bungalow at no 182 now stands was The Lodge to Eastwick Park where Mr Dicker, gardener/gatekeeper, and his wife lived until a German bomb destroyed it with a direct hit on 24 October 1941. Thankfully, they were both taken out of the wreckage unhurt. About a week after the direct hit on The Lodge a land mine fell in the grounds north of Southey Hall and after further bombs dropped near the school, staff and pupils were evacuated. The Canadian Army then occupied the building for the rest of the war.

In 1946 the school returned to Southey Hall but it closed in 1954. Shortly afterwards Eastwick Park/Southey Hall was demolished and it is understood that two lion statues that were at Eastwick Park now grace the front of Headley House, Headley. Little else remains of the past at Eastwick but parts of the moat survive, off Eastwick Park Avenue, as does part of the kitchen garden wall in the grounds of Southey Court.

Southey Court is a residential home, run by Mole Valley District Council, which is also off Eastwick Park Avenue. It was opened in

Southey Hall School in 1950

1989 and is set in some beautiful surroundings. A number of the residents of Southey Court have helped me with my researches into the recent history of Bookham. Adjacent to Southey Court is Keswick House which was built in 1973 by Surrey County Council for the aged who are unable to take care of themselves. It is now run by the Anchor Trust. Bookham Youth Centre is in this part of the village. It was built by the county council and opened in 1969.

On the other side of Lower Road is the 17th century inn, The Anchor. At the early part of the 20th century it was sold by William Keswick to the Swan Brewery Company, Leatherhead when it had a public bar, tap room and a parlour. Percy Burnham was landlord of The Anchor for 31 years, retiring in 1990 and ending his days little more than a hundred yards from the pub in a cottage in Eastwick Road. During the 1960s Christine Keeler stayed at The Anchor during the Profumo trial.

On the opposite corner of Eastwick Road is the 16th/17th century house, half timber and brick, that was Woodcote. In the early 1900s Mr Poulter had a horse and cart transport business that operated from Woodcote to and from London twice a week. The house is now divided into two properties. Adjoining is a barn where the Eastwick farm bull was kept.

Next, in Eastwick Road, are Albert Cottages where two branches of the Stemp family lived. James Stemp lived at no 1 as a boy and much later had the saddlery next to the Royal Oak. Turville Kille and his newly wed wife, Annie (née Stemp), lived in two rooms at no 2 when they were first married.

At the beginning of the century William Keswick built thirteen houses on the east side of the road, south of the Anchor, for his farm and estate workers. These were part of a self contained unit which included a school, a laundry and a nurse's home. The school was not introduced by Keswick since a plot of land on the west side of Eastwick Road, known as Chilman's Field, was sold in 1830 and a National School was built on the site and enlarged in 1882. By 1907 the school had become in such a poor condition and was so overcrowded that it was sold by the trustees in 1910 and was incorporated into the new part of St James School. Mrs Hewitt continued to run the Eastwick School privately until at least 1916 when, on marrying a worker on the Eastwick estate, she closed her school. The school buildings still survive and the two houses which front on to Eastwick Road are named The Old School House and Chilman's Lea. The small two-storey building at the back was the music room.

Turville Kille was born at the house called The Homestead in

1898 when his father worked at the Eastwick Farm. In 1911 the Kille family moved into what had been the school building. Later, there was a further move by the Kille family to Ralph's Cottage at the junction of Crabtree Lane and Leatherhead Road. George White was born at the Homestead in 1916 but his family moved to Victoria Hall when the house was taken over by Walter Finch. In 1915 Mr Finch moved with his family from Sussex to Hill House Farm on Bookham Common. By 1924 he had saved sufficient money to be able to place a deposit on The Homestead and the farm buildings on the west side of Eastwick Road which had previously been part of the Eastwick Park Estate. It was here where he started a cartage business, commencing with the transportation of building materials from the station to the various building sites that were opening up in Bookham. Finch was the main contractor in the construction of the Church Road telephone exchange in 1932 and he was able to provide storage for materials and accommodation for the workers on his property. He also carried coal supplies from the station to the village. After the Second World War the firm began to concentrate on transporting heavy machinery, particularly dry cleaning machines made by Neil and Spencer. The business has continued to change and expand through four generations of the family. Walter died in 1963, his son 'Snowy' continued with the business until his death in 1981 and two further generations, Richard and Andrew, continue to successfully run the Finch business. The farm buildings, that were set out in a U formation, remain almost unchanged and the stables, blacksmith's shop, carpenter's and wheelwright's shop, cart sheds, piggery and barn are all now used as offices and storage by various enterprises, but the house is still residential.

The Congregational Church on the corner of Eastwick Road and Keswick Road that opened in 1929 is now the Bookham United Reformed Church. They had previously used a corrugated iron hall in Church Road. Keswick Road was, until the early 1920s, part of a footpath between East Street and Lower Road. Greville Court is built on a marl pit in which Keswick introduced a modern form of sanitation to the Hamlet by running the sewage through pipes from the houses in Eastwick Road and St Nicholas Avenue into the bottom of the disused pit. Some forty years later, during World War II, the Home Guard and the Canadian troops used the pit as a firing range. The pit had been disused for a very long time when, in 1972, it was filled in and Greville Court was built using piled foundations. Alongside Greville Court on the corner of Durleston Park Drive is the Guide Headquarters which was opened around 1970.

On the corner of Keswick Road and Eastwick Road are the allotments which have been here from the late 1800s. At Keswick's death the allotment ground was put up for sale and the area where the Beckley shops are was sold but fortunately the remainder of the ground was not. It would seem that Turville Kille was partly instrumental in persuading Epsom Council to buy the land and so saved the allotments.

Hops and wheat had been grown on the land to the west of Eastwick Road. The bungalows were built in the early 1920s but the rest of the land remained as Eastwick Nursery. The nursery was originally run by Mr Guilbert and it remained as a nursery under various owners until the 1950s. The roads in the first development here are Proctor Gardens and Candy Croft, both named after previous doctors in the village. In 1977/8 the rest of the land was developed and Turville Court is named after one of Bookham's best known characters.

Passed The Anchor at St Nicholas Avenue the houses were built by Keswick to accommodate his higher grade employees. The style and sizes of these semi-detached houses vary suggesting that allocation of these houses depended on the level or rank of the occupier and or the size of his family. This is a road which has changed very little over the past hundred years.

Returning to Lower Road and turning right Eastwick Cottage is on the right hand side of the road. This has had some additions but it is a 15th century house.

Until the 1920s the only house in Lower Road between here and the Ridgeway was Eastwick House, on the corner of what is now Lower Road and Eastwick Drive. It was the second farm that belonged to Eastwick Park and was previously known as Eastwick Park Farm and later as Home Farm. The house is virtually unchanged and some of the original stables that back on to Lower Road remain, used as garages, but other farm buildings were destroyed in a fire in 1930. Originally there was a farm gate across what is now Eastwick Drive at its junction with Lower Road and a track led to the service entrance of the Eastwick estate which was roughly where the school entrance is today. This was where the building was which housed the electric generator for the house. The cart track continued northwards and reduced to a footpath, which went over the level crossing (until it was closed in 1924), and across Bookham Common to Stoke D'Abernon. This track became Eastwick Drive and it began to be developed from the 1920s Almost opposite Eastwick House are the remains of the dairy buildings of Eastwick Park. Two hexagonal shaped brick buildings, built around 1810, one of which was a dairy, the other a scalding house were joined by an enclosed corridor; they were originally thatched but they are now roofed with decorative tiles.

Just a few yards on is a cul-de-sac called The Spinney which is the site of The Spinney Preparatory School which was here from 1930 until 1967. When the Eastwick Estate was broken up and sold in the 1920s a two acre site was bought on which the Scarlett bungalows in Lower Road were built on the south and Eastwick Drive was to the east. Within the site were three large barns that had been cowsheds and the one nearest to Eastwick Drive was converted by the owner to a two-storey house fronting Eastwick Drive. Miss Dorothy Joce, her sister and mother bought the site in 1930 to use the house and two barns for a preparatory school. The school was named after a nearby chestnut spinney. As the Spinney Preparatory School grew, with Dorothy Joce as headmistress, the barns were modified and added to. The school became very popular with local people wishing their children to have a private education. In 1950 Miss Linday, the senior mistress, took over the School and Miss Joce retired. She went to live at Foxmead, a very large house in Maddox Lane. The Spinney ceased to be a boarding school and Miss Joce arranged for the few children that could not return home each day to be boarded at Foxmead. In 1967 the Spinney School moved to Merrylands Farm, Church Road and the ground at Eastwick Drive was sold enabling the present cul-de-sac to be built. In 1980 the Spinney school was absorbed into Manor House school in Little Bookham.

On the east side of Eastwick Drive three of the five bungalows that were built in the late 1920s retain the original park railings along their frontage, as have other properties on this side of the road. Further on, where Richmond Way is there was a horticultural nursery run by Mr Hendriksen until the early 1960s when he was bought out in preparation for housing development. He continues to operate nurseries near Hatchford Park and on the Isle of Wight.

Turning into Eastwick Park Avenue, adjacent to the footpath to Park View, are Bookham's passenger-carrying trolley buses. These are in the garden of Peter Lepine-Smith. The vehicles, which are occasionally driven around the garden, are one-third scale models built on chassis from Job's Dairy milk floats fed from overhead conductors. There are three trolleybuses based on Reading Corporation vehicles kept in the depot with its workshop and sub-station.

Trolley buses in Eastwick Park Avenue.

The house by the ponds, on the corner of Long Copse, near Eastwick Drive, was a gamekeeper's cottage for the estate. Roads like Spring Grove, Richmond Way and others were built in the very long gardens which were with the houses in Kennel Lane. A little further on the left hand side is the house known as Commons End where Mr and Mrs Harrison lived who did so much for the Bookham Community Association.

The crossroads with Meadowside on the left and Meadow Way on the right were originally part of a path that led to the station. Until the early 1970s Meadow Way was linked to The Copse by a short footpath as a result of development taking place from two different directions, but although not everyone wanted it the two roads were eventually joined. A little further on the left side of The Copse there was, up until the mid 1970s, a pig farm at the rear of the bungalow where the road curves rather sharply known as Sunnymead Farm. At the last property on the right in Eastwick Drive, Covehithe, Mr Riley ran a poultry farm between 1925 and 1950.

The level crossing here was closed in 1924; in the road on the other side of the line, Commonside, the first property was Parslow's Hamster Farm which operated here for many years until the 1980s. Beyond that is Keeper's Cottage, another house left

72

from the Eastwick Park estate.

On the corner of Lower Road and Amey Drive (named after Mrs Emily Amey of Victoria Cottage, High Street), is a house called Durleston. This was the home of Sir George Edwards in the 1960s and 70s. He had joined Vickers at Weybridge in 1935 and retired in 1975 as Chairman of British Aircraft Corporation. Continuing eastwards along Lower Road on the left hand side is Kennel Lane named after the home of the Surrey Union Hounds around the beginning of the last century. The kennels were about where Sayers Close is now. In the 1930s there were plans for an orbital road to run from Givons Grove close to the Bookham-Fetcham boundary to Stoke D'Abernon. Land was reserved for this until the 1970s and it was not released for development until the M25 had been constructed in 1986.

CHAPTER 7

Leatherhead Road

On the south side of Leatherhead Road there was, until around the end of the 20th century, a shop housing The Victory Press. This printing works was opened by Fred Barford when he took over an existing shop early in the 1930s. Fred died in 1951 and the printing works closed in the 1970s. Roughly opposite the press in a house called Cyssandi there was a preparatory school during the 1930s. Nearby, in the 1920s, a dwelling called Mandara, was occupied by Wing Commander Mead who ran a poultry farm at the rear of his property that reached as far as Keswick Road. A little further on, H R Richmond had a coach business at Dagshai before moving to their Epsom depot.

On the south side of the road is P M Clack & Son, timber merchants. Mr Clack came from Beddington to Bookham in the early 1920s and sct up his builder's merchants and timber business

Gilmais swimming pool in the 1930s.

here. The firm has passed to son and then grandson but still operates in the same yard.

Directly opposite Clack's is the close named Gilmais. From the early 1930s Gilmais house and grounds contained a popular social club with an open air swimming pool and tennis courts. It was opened and owned by Gilbert and Maisie White, hence Gil Mais. He was a test pilot who tragically crashed and was killed just after the outbreak of war in 1939. The pool and courts remained open until around 1961 when it was sold and the road now called Gilmais was built. The White's house still stands in Gilmais, between its newer neighbours.

Beckley Cottages until the 1920s stood on their own except for Ralph's Cottage and the buildings in Flint Close. From 1920 until the outbreak of the Second World War Mr and Mrs Pelling and their family lived in Beckley Cottage, the double fronted cottage at the end of the row. Mrs Pelling was the daughter of Andrew West, the local builder.

Henry Griffiths, who had been the blind organist and choir master at Bookham Church and musical director at the Leatherhead School for the Blind for many years, lived at no 7 Beckley Cottages. In the early 1930s Henry was offered a BBC job on the radio but he refused because he thought that 'radio was not going to last'! Henry's son Geoff tells of life here in the 1920s and 1930s when the well behind the cottages was superseded by one tap for all the cottages and when two spinsters in one of the cottages refused a gas supply and preferred oil lamps as they were safer.

Little or no development took place south of Leatherhead Road before the early 1920s when the number of plots of land being bought began to increase and properties were built, many of which were small inexpensive bungalows. Better quality houses began to appear after a few years and most of these survive. According to Turville Kille, in some cases squatter's rights were used to obtain some of these plots of ground. Unlike the Scarlett bungalows elsewhere in the village most properties here were individually built, there were no estates until the 1950s. Downsway and Crabtree Lane had previously been footpaths and as development took place the roads were left unmade. In wet weather this resulted in the roads becoming a quagmire and there are stories told of delivery vehicles being up to their axles in mud. Hard surfaces were not laid until the mid 1930s, the road making being carried out by unemployed Welshmen imported to the district. The increase in house construction in south Bookham brought shops to the area, among the earliest in the Beckley parade were the Bungalow Stores, Blackmore's haberdashery and ironmongery shop and the newsagents.

The two garages came here in the 1920s. Gau and Lawes was where Hylands Garage is and Brookes Garage where Beckley garage is today. Where the UCS motor accessory suppliers is there used to be the Guildford and District Co-operative store, also built in the 1920s. It was a single storey building until the 1950s when the first floor was added; between the co-op shop and the garage was the Co-operative Hall which was used for social functions. The shops in New Parade were built in the 1930s and are now occupied by the off-license and the fried fish shop. Over the years there have been chemists, grocers, an electrical shop barber, a laundrette, an angling store, and Bookham Ironmongers among the occupants of these shops.

During the last war the Auxiliary Fire Service, later the National Fire Service, had a sub-station at the Gau and Lawes garage and Turville Kille was made section leader and put in charge of the Bookham sub-section of the Leatherhead brigade. After a bomb had fallen on what is now Michael's fish shop a prefabricated hut was erected on the site for the firemen.

Mrs Wooton started The Beckley Rabbitry in 1941 at 1 Beckley Parade which she shared with the off-license. It was an attempt to encourage families to keep rabbits to help with the meat ration, this enterprise continued throughout the war.

Turville Kille lived with his wife Annie at Downsview, the house next door to the fish shop, from 1925 until her death in 1982. After his wife's death he continued to live there for another 12 years before moving to Southey Court.

At the beginning of the 20th century an unfortunate tragedy occurred in a field at the south end of Crabtree Lane. A balloon that had travelled from Crystal Palace came down and several local men held the balloon down by its ropes while more gas was pumped into it. When sufficient gas had been supplied the order to let go of the ropes was given but 'Ticky' Tickner, who lived in one of the Flint Cottages, failed to hear the order and was dragged up with the balloon as it rose and he fell to his death.

On the south east corner of Downsway is the house where Mr and Mrs Macdonald had their hairdressers' business, after they moved from the Victoria Hotel, until they retired in the 1990s. On the other corner of Downsway was the attractive Corner House Restaurant that was open from the 1930s to the 1950s.

On the south west corner of Crabtree Lane is the three-storey Ralph's Cottages which date from the late 19th century. These have been known locally as Sparrow Barracks for some unknown reason. It is believed that it was at this junction that the body of Ralph Sutherland was buried after he was hanged at the gallows here for sheep rustling at Polesden Lacey in the early part of the 18th century. It is understood that human bones were found when digging took place here some time ago. Turville Kille lived at Ralph's Cottages as a very young man after his family moved from The School House in Eastwick Road. His mother ran a successful hand laundry at Ralph's Cottage employing a number of laundry workers during and following the First World War.

Next to Ralph's Cottage in Crabtree Lane is a narrow long-established footpath that leads to the south end of Flint Close and on to Dorking Road. Between Flint Close and Southend there were several single-storey residences known locally as the Black Huts because they were timber with a bitumen covering to make them waterproof. Alongside the Black Huts there were Flint Cottages which had bare earth floors. One of these cottages consisted of two semi-detached houses that shared a single staircase and it was in one of these that Emily and William Amey lived for a while before they moved to 28 High Street. Surprisingly both Flint Cottages and the Black Huts survived and were occupied until 1960, when the Council replaced them with the present houses.

At the end of Flint Close there are a number of houses, some of which were built in the late 19th century. The Rt Hon Sir Bartle Frere had been a leading colonial administrator and Governor of Bombay and on his staff was Surgeon Major Frederic Savignac Stedman who had lived at Fairfield in Lower Road. In the late 1880s Stedman bought land to the south of Leatherhead Road, where Flint Close is, and built a block of four almshouses on it, each having two rooms up and two rooms down. He later built an extension of two more houses and named them Frere Cottages in memory of his patron. A plaque on the front of the house records:

Frere House Cottages were built and endowed in 1889 for the benefit of aged women by Surgeon Major Stedman of the Bombay Army and of Fairfield, Great Bookham. In memory of the late Right Honourable Sir Bartle Frere, Governor of Bombay.

In the 1960s a further block of four almshouses was built, named Hughes House, after a Bookham Rector. They were placed on trust to accommodate 'ladies in need' who had lived in Great Bookham for two years. With the consent of the Charities Commission this has been extended to include ladies from Mole

Valley or elsewhere. The almshouses were not endowed but three other charities benefit Great Bookham and their donations have been used to support the almshouses. In 1936 the Charities Commission produced a scheme which unified the administration of the four charities, hence the name Bookham United Charities. The trusts are administered by the Frere Trustees: the Rector of Great Bookham as ex-officio chairman, two nominated by the Mole Valley District Council, one nominated by the Stedman Family and three co-opted for their expertise.

On the north west corner of Eastwick Road and Leatherhead Road is a bungalow in which lives a ninety plus year old gentleman, Mr Charles Bowles. He has lived there for 27 years and told me that after World War I a demobbed soldier, as part of an aid scheme, was offered the use of an ex-army hut, that had been brought from London, plus a plot of ground on which to run a poultry farm but unfortunately it failed financially. A builder bought the plot and the hut and extended and developed the hut to what it is today. One can still see at the front of the house the outline of that original hut. The two gentlemen who were living at the bungalow in 1939 had an air raid shelter built in the back garden that contained three bunk beds, an air filter, mains electricity and an escape hatch. The shelter still survives. When Mr Bowles moved here in 1970 he found that the shelter was almost full of wine bottles, some of which still had wine in them, as a previous owner used the shelter as a wine cellar.

A little further west there was the Woodman Nursery which since the 1970s has been occupied by the two bungalows Woodman and Breage. Even further west there is what used to be two police houses and a police office until the 1970s.

The Fairfield was an area of about 3 acres where fairs would have been held in past times for the sale of cattle, foodstuffs and clothing. It was originally part of the Eastwick estate and the houses built by Epsom council in the 1920s (Fairfield Cottages) are on part of it and the rest was owned by Stephen Worrel, the High Street butcher. In 1956 the 'S' bend was removed from the main road so that it now goes right in front of Fairfield Cottages in a straight line with Guildford Road. On the south side of the road there is an estate of bungalows in Leatherhead Road and Allen Road. This is the Bookham Manor estate which was built in 1957 on the site of Bookham Cottage, a chalet bungalow built in 1914, the last occupant of which was Herbert Allen, a builder, who had ten children, five boys and five girls.

The footpath to the recreation ground was between Bookham Cottage and The Paddocks, a large detached house which stood in large grounds. In 1897 Mrs Chrystie bought The Paddocks and gave a part of the grounds to the village as a recreation ground, which the parish council later extended to its present size. In 1933, helped by some unemployed men of the village, a bowling green was laid out by Mr Longhurst, the gardener from Church Road. This work was organised by the Bookham Social Services Bureau financed by local people and traders. Adolph Schloesser and his family lived in The Paddocks from the beginning of the century until about 1917 during which time his two daughters ran a penny library for the village. The Paddocks had been used in its latter years as an apartment house, but it was demolished in 1971 and the present Paddocks estate built.

Opposite The Paddocks, on the triangular green under the trees, there is a considerable rise in the ground. This is where the local council buried a Second World War air raid shelter and planted trees around it. Between the triangular green and Croftlands Cottage is the part of East Street that was isolated when Leatherhead Road was straightened. Croftlands Cottage and Cherry Tree Cottage were built in the first years of the 20th century for the estate workers of Bookham Grove. Although of simple two up-two down construction these cottages were built with cavity walls. The wall around these houses is part of the original wall of the Saracen and Ring inn.

A few yards along Dorking Road on the left hand side there is a gateway in the flint wall leading to a recently-built house. Until the spring of 1998 a bungalow, built in 1920–30, called Paddocks Cottage stood on this site. In the 1930s Mr Brackenbury senior, a builder, lived there with his family until 1939 when they moved to the High Street. Paddocks Cottage was occupied by Mr and Mrs Marks from the late sixties. I shall never forget my visit to them one day in 1994. I knocked at the front door but immediately realised that it was not possible because of its decrepit condition to open the door and so I walked around the side of the house, tapped on the glass window of the side door and was invited into the sitting room by Mr Marks. Mrs Marks a frail little old lady who was both blind and deaf was unable to communicate with me. Sadly Mr Marks died in the early part of 1998 and his widow went to live in Keswick House where she was very happy. Within a very short time Paddocks Cottage was sold and demolished and in its place there now stands a modern house. Further on, on the left

Bookham Grove before World War II.

are riding stables. Until the early 1920s the Surrey Union Hounds, who hunted on Tuesdays and Saturdays, were kennelled here after they moved from Kennel Lane.

At the corner of Dorking Road and Lower Shott is the impressive house, Bookham Grove. Built before 1720, when it was known as Grove House, the Guildford-Leatherhead Road was diverted to improve the entrance to the house and this remained until 1956. The grounds at the front of the house then extended to Guildford Road over the present car park. The brick-built, single storey building to the left of the entrance to Bookham Grove was where the stables were. Part of this building was the public library from 1958 until they moved to the old school building in 1988. Originally the grounds of Bookham Grove covered some forty acres including a farm and the Saracen and Ring inn. In 1895 Mrs Chrystie bought the inn, closed it and resold it as a dwelling house with the name Grove Cottage. The Dawnay family had held the title deeds of Bookham Grove until 1909 when Mrs Silverberg bought the house, the farm and Grove Cottages. During the First World War she and her husband changed their name to Hayward when people with German sounding names were treated with suspicion.

In February 1922 there appeared in many prominent places throughout the village a small poster advertising the fact that there was to be a meeting to discuss the holding of a Gigantic Fete, Bazaar and County Fair from which money would be raised to finance a number of urgently needed projects in the parish church. The heating system and the organ both needed replacing and there was a need of a choir vestry. The total cost was estimated to be £1000 and the village set about raising this large sum. The rector, the Rev G S Bird, was made president of the fete, Stanley Russell was elected chairman, C W Todd was Treasurer and Mrs Russell and Harold Bostock were joint secretaries. A number of well-known people in the district accepted an invitation to become patrons. An executive panel of under 30 people and a large general committee of about 80 were formed which enabled preparation for the mighty event to begin including advertising using posters, the local papers and the parish magazine. A number of functions were organised to pay for the fete expenses including jumble sales, whist and bridge drives, tennis tournaments and concerts by schoolchildren. During the spring the committees met regularly and, as he would be staying at Polesden Lacey at the time, Stanley Russell asked whether the Duke of York would graciously consent to attend the fete and to everyone's delight he agreed to do so which must have contributed immensely towards the success of the event. There were to be 12 stalls, each directed by prominent members of the village, among whom were Mrs Stanley Russell, Mrs Sidney Madge, Mrs P Everitt, Mr and Mrs Griffin, Mr H P Roe and Mr and Mrs Stevens. The East Surrey Regimental Band was booked to play throughout the 3 days and there was the County Fair consisting of steam-driven roundabouts, swings, coconut shies, hooplas, etc. Perhaps most surprising was the offer of a neighbouring meadow, owned by Mr D Val Reid, as a car park to accommodate up to a 1000 cars. On Monday 19th June the weather was perfect and Lord and Lady Ashcombe arrived at midday to open the Fete. At 12.30 the Duke of York arrived with his hostess, Mrs Greville and toured the various stalls and rode on one of the roundabouts. Just before the duke left the fete Richard Ragge, 90 years of age and the oldest parishioner, who had run the harness and leather shop in the High Street for the greater part of his life, was presented to him. After the departure of the duke, the crowds continued to pour into the fete with the blazing sunshine reflecting off the many great white marquees and highlighting the brilliant colours of the dresses of the stallholders. The takings at the end of the first day were £370, the second day £220 and the third day yielded £320 and so the total sum for the three days exceeded the £1000 target that had been set. As a mark of appreciation for his efforts Stanley Russell was presented with an illuminated address signed by all members of the executive committee and the rector.

The following year the Duke and Duchess of York spent part of their honeymoon at Polesden Lacey during which they attended

Sunday morning service at St. Nicolas church much to the delight of the villagers.

Mrs Hayward lived at Bookham Grove until 1947, when the Leatherhead Urban District Council took over the estate and divided the house in to flats allowing the beautiful spiral Regency staircase in the very attractive entrance hall to remain. The Grove estate was built in the surrounding grounds. Later the house was sold to a developer who built some houses alongside the mansion.

The two semi-detached cottages, now known as 1 and 2 Grove Cottages, had previously been a coaching inn, The Saracen and Ring. Coachmen from Leatherhead chose to come to Bookham along Lower Road to avoid Hawks Hill and would sound their post horn as they approached the inn along the High Street. The inn was given the name in commemoration of an action of an ancestor of Viscount Downe, Sir William Dawnay, during the Crusades. Apart from a small addition to one side of the house, which is now divided into two, there are no significant changes from the days when it was an inn. While visiting no 2 I was shown by Margaret Clements, the occupier, the wooden door opening at the side of the cottage through which barrels were lowered into the cellar. The interior of the cottage retains a picturesque quaintness.

At Grove Cottages you may look across to Rayleigh House where these walks started. I hope that they have enabled you to learn more about the Bookhams during the last century.

Further Reading

S E D Fortescue *People and Places, Great and Little Bookham* S E D Fortescue, 1978
S E D Fortescue *The Story of Two Villages, Great and Little Bookham,* S E D Fortescue, 1975
Linda Heath (comp) *Bookham and Fetcham,* Tempus, 1999
Christine Leonard *Golden Jubilee of the Bookham Community Association,* B.C.A. 1998
Peter Tarplee *A Guide to the Industrial History of Mole Valley District,* S.I.H.G, 1998
Wendy Young *Turville: the life and times of Turville Kille and Stories of Old Bookham from 1898,* Turville Kille, 1998